Get Your Book Seen and Sold

The Essential Publishing and Book Marketing Guide

Claudine Wolk
Julie Murkette

Lost Valley Press
an imprint of Satya House Publications

Copyright ©2023 by Claudine Wolk and Julie Murkette
Lost Valley Press
an imprint of Satya House Publications
P. O. Box 122
Hardwick, MA 01037

lostvalleypress.com
lostvalleypress@gmail.com

All rights reserved. No part of this book may be reproduced or utilized in any form or by any means, electronic or mechanical, including photocopying, recording, or by any information storage retrieval system, with the exception of a reviewer who may quote brief passages in a review, without permission in writing from the publisher. The publisher and author disclaim any personal liability, directly or indirectly, for advice or information presented within. Although the author and publisher have made every effort to ensure the accuracy and completeness of the information contained within, we assume no responsibility for errors, inaccuracies, omissions or inconsistencies.

ISBN: 978-1-935874-44-7 print
ISBN: 978-1-935874-46-1 eBook

Library of Congress Control Number: 2023940175

Book Cover Design by ILMC Designs

TABLE OF CONTENTS

Introduction 5

Part One

Your Publishing Choices: Traditional and Self-Publishing 9

Part Two

Marketing and Promotion 31

Message, Audience, Hook - Oh My! 36

Marketing Tools: Meet the Media Kit 60

Marketing Plan: Plus THE SECRET 74

Distinctive Book Marketing Ideas 89

Exhibits 105

Why Us? About the Authors 119

INTRODUCTION

You wrote a book and you want to publish it. That's the first step. Congratulations!

We have some simple questions that will help you decide **how to publish** before we even have to talk about the **different ways there are** to publish.

1. Do you want to get your book in the hands of a **few select people**: your family and your friends, for example? Perhaps you own a business and you wrote the book specifically for your customers?

OR

2. Do you want your book to reach every reader out there? Do you want your book to be available in every bookstore — online or brick-and-mortar? Do you want your book in libraries? Do you want your book to be a trade paperback? Do you want your book to be an eBook and an audio book as well as a paperback and/or hardcover? Do you want your book to sit alongside every trade book out there?

These are important questions because there are very different ways to publish and sell your book that depend on your answer. **Put simply...**

If you plan to sell to a select group (family, friends, customers), you can publish a print book or/and create an eBook fairly quickly in just a couple of months. **However...** if you plan to sell your book like any other traditionally published book in existence — and give it the same shot to sell as any other trade book—it will take more time to publish and release your book... **as long as a year.**

STOP

Please re-read the previous sentence. It is critical for the success of your book for you to understand the timing involved.

WHY A YEAR?

If you plan to sell your book to the world, the world needs time to **learn about your book before your actual publication date.** The book industry wants 4 to 9 months in advance to check out your book and potentially review it. After you've finished writing your manuscript, add 3 or 4 months for someone (other than you) to edit and design your book and cover. This is prior to the time that the book industry needs to review your book. So you are looking at a year! Whew! Breathe. A year seems like a long time, especially if you want your book released tomorrow. We will explain the process a few different ways so that you can absorb why it takes as long as a year.

> ### WHAT'S A GALLEY?
> A galley is a "review copy" of your book. Also referred to as an Advance Reader Copy (ARC), it is your bound manuscript (it could also be an eGalley) with a special back cover filled with marketing and publicity information. The review copy does not have to be the final version of the book, but close enough for reviewers to review it!

The following example of the timing of book publishing is true for a self-publisher or a traditional publisher. For ease of understanding, we describe a self-publisher.

As an example of the timing of publishing, set a release date in your mind. Let's pick September as a release date (a popular release date, btw). Now count back nine months to January!

January is when the book must be essentially completed. It may seem crazy, but it's true! Your book must be written, edited, with an interior design and a book cover design by January so that you can submit it to the industry and other reviewers (in galley/ARC form) who need several months to review your book.

Introduction: Before You Read Anything Else

That means you have to start your work in September! Why September? September gives you three months (plus time off for the holidays) until January to complete the essential elements of your book: editing, interior design, and book cover creation.

Said another way, if you finish your manuscript in September of any given year, you could **consider** a September pub date in the following year.

Do not panic. We just threw a lot of information at you. What is important to know right now is the importance of the **timing** of your publication and release date. You don't want to rush the release date of your book and miss out on the opportunity of the exposure of industry book reviewers.

> FYI, industry book reviewers provide VERY specific and unique instructions to submit a review copy to them. The best chance for a look at your book is to follow those instructions to the letter!

A TYPICAL PUBLISHING TIMELINE

Complete manuscript, edit, interior design, book cover design (September to January)

Create galley, research media contacts and reviewers, develop Marketing Plan (January - April)

Send review copies to industry reviewers (April)

Final books printed and/or eBook file created (July) in advance of publication date.

Publication Date (September)

To summarize, if you decide that you want your book to be a trade book — available everywhere you buy books — you must consider the timing of your publication to be spread out over a year. You will have three months to review the manuscript, edit it, create the interior design and create the book cover. Once the book is completed, you will send a review copy of the book to industry reviewers who require the book prior to publication. You wait for the reviews to come back, put the finishing touches on the book, create and begin to implement your Marketing Plan, print the final copies, send the final copies to distributors and then formally publish, a year AFTER you started!

Are you excited at the prospect of publishing YOUR book? Great! Let's move on to decide HOW to publish your book!

PART ONE

Your Publishing Choices: Traditional and Self-Publishing

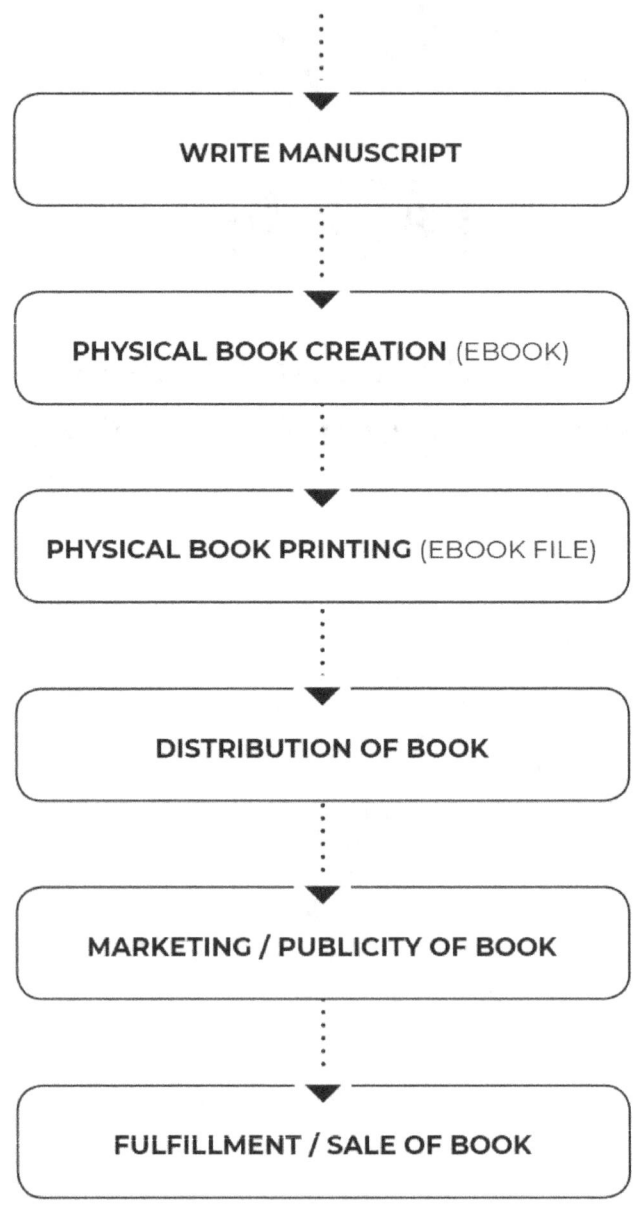

Your Publishing Choices

Since you have decided that you want to publish a trade paperback (and eBook) and get it into the hands of as many people as possible, you now have to decide HOW you will publish.

You can commercially-publish (traditional publisher) or self-publish. There are variations and hybrids of each type of publishing, but we want to make it as simple as we can for you to decide what is best for you and your book. We will describe each briefly and then include "responsibility" flow charts that will highlight the publisher's responsibility for each publishing task and YOUR responsibility for each publishing task under both options to make it easier for you to decide.

First, have a look at the *Publishing Flowchart* on the opposite page. Although you have two publishing choices, the tasks for each publisher are essentially the same. In this first *Publishing Flowchart* exhibit, you can get a good idea of the publishing tasks required to get your book published. As we describe each of your choices, we'll present another publishing flowchart that highlights the tasks for each of the steps and highlight who must perform the task under each publishing scenario.

TRADITIONAL PUBLISHER

Our guess is that you are already familiar with traditional publishers. If you watched the hit TV series *Younger* where two of the lead characters work for a publishing company, you have seen a traditional publisher in action. Like the fictional publisher in the show, *Empirical,* the traditional publisher seeks out books to publish, presents offers to authors, creates the book, edits the book, designs the book and the book cover, distributes the book and markets the book. The publisher OWNS the book. The publisher prints, distributes and sells the book.

The author, in a traditional publishing deal, gets an advance of money up front and then a **percentage** of net (yes, net — not gross) book sales. However, the author only gets the percentage of net sales of books payment when the original advance is "paid back" to the publisher through book sales. After the entire advance is "paid back" — ala book sales — the author will get a percentage of net sales in a payment, also called a book royalty, and usually paid per quarter. You have guessed by now that many, many books must be sold to make money as an author with a traditional publisher over and above the initial author advance. Net sales are generally determined this way: Retail price of book minus print cost minus seller's discount minus distributor's fees. For example: the publisher sets the retail price of your book at $20. Book sellers (bookstores, Amazon, etc.) generally get a 45-55% discount off the retail price when they purchase the book to sell. For ease of mathematics, let's say they get a 50% discount, bringing us to $10. Depending on the publisher and the distributor, they will take 22-27% of the $10 to cover their fees. Again, for ease of mathematics, let's call it 22%. That brings us to $7.80. Let's say it costs $4 per copy to print. Now we're down to $3.80. The distributor and/or publisher may also charge for storage (usually 1 cent per copy per month), as well as some advertising fees. We think you get the picture.

Good News: money paid up front to you, no money paid out to produce the book, no fulfillment of sales responsibility or accounting headache, the prestige of being an author with a publishing house.

Bad News: You do not own the book, your % of net sales payment is low and you are STILL expected to do a substantial amount of work (including money outlay) to market and publicize your book.

As you can see from the *Traditional Publishing Flowchart*, there are some tasks that you do and some tasks that they do. For a traditional publisher in the publishing process, they do more than you do (more light grey tasks than dark grey tasks). However, your job of marketing and publicity for your books never really ends and traditional publishers expect you to be fully engaged in the publicity of your book. Don't worry! Part Two of this workbook will make you an expert in marketing your book! On to your next choice!

PUBLISHING FLOWCHART

Traditional Publishing Tasks

You Do: Dark Grey
They Do: Light Grey

Manuscript Word Doc

Book Interior Layout

Book Cover: Front, Back, Spine

CIP
ISBN
Barcode
QR Code

Editing
Proofreading

Index

Physical Book Printing

Ebook File Creation

Distribution to 3rd Party Distributors

Upload Ebook to Online Platforms

Galley / Review Copy
Publicist
Press materials

Website
Online Pitching
Social Media
Interviews

Ship Books to Distributors & Book Buyers

Record Sales of Ebooks

SELF-PUBLISHING

Self-publishing is when YOU create your own publishing company and publish your own book. We know it sounds daunting and there is work to be done, but it is not as difficult as you may think. Before we get into to details of self-publishing, read my (Claudine's) story.

I self-published my first book. I was where you are in the decision-making process when I had a "lightbulb" moment. I was reading the definitive tome on self-publishing, *Dan Poynter's Self-Publishing Manual*, in my quest to move forward on my first manuscript, *It Gets Easier and Other Lies We Tell New Mothers*. I was reading the famous red book while sitting on bleachers at a field during my son's lacrosse practice when it hit me. This book managed to get it through my thick skull that if I self-publish, I would actually be publishing traditionally! The only difference was that **I** would be the publisher.

My book would look the same as a book published by Harper Collins. The book would be a trade paperback with all of the industry standard elements of any other published book. The book would not be published by Claudine Wolk, but by my new publishing company — New Buck Press. LIGHTBULB! I didn't have to wait for a publisher or agent to accept and produce my book. Additionally, the industry book buyers (distributors, bookstores, libraries, online bookstores, etc.) would purchase my industry-standard book the standard way, through the publisher — New Buck Press. Reviewers would be notified of the book's existence through the publisher, New Buck Press, and so on. You get the idea.

The understanding was a revelation. I could publish the book myself without it looking like I was publishing it myself. Plus, by publishing myself, I was not closing the door to a publishing contract with a traditional publisher down the road. Sometimes the big firms simply need to see that a book can garner sales before they invest, which happened with my book. That is a story for another time.

Your Publishing Choices

PUBLISHING FLOWCHART
Self-Publishing Tasks

You Do: Grey

Manuscript Word Doc

- Book Interior Layout
- Book Cover: Front, Back, Spine
- CIP / ISBN / Barcode / QR Code
- Editing / Proofreading
- Index

- Physical Book Printing
- Ebook File Creation

- Distribution to 3rd Party Distributors
- Upload Ebook to Online Platforms

- Galley / Review Copy / Publicist / Press materials
- Website / Online Pitching / Social Media / Interviews

- Ship Books to Distributors & Book Buyers
- Record Sales of Ebooks

If you self-publish, YOU produce the book. You write it, you edit it, you create the interior design, you design the book cover, you produce the finished digital file of the book and book cover for the printer, and you produce the digital file for the eBook according to the specifications of the eBook sellers with whom you choose to do business. OR…you can sub-contract out the parts you aren't comfortable doing yourself. We do advise having someone other than yourself edit the book and then proofread the final version before it goes to print. You've been looking at it for so long as you've been writing it, you will probably miss things that a fresh set of eyes will see immediately.

Once the book is ready to be sold, you fulfill the book sales yourself. Fulfillment means that you will invoice book purchasers, collect payment, ship the books to the purchasers, and pay sales tax to the proper entities. You are required to keep track of your sales and expenses related to your publishing company and report your net earnings to the IRS at tax time.

You are also in charge of marketing and publicity. You (or someone you hire) will create a Press Release and other Media Kit items (author bio, one-page sell sheet, interview Q&A, announcement postcards, etc.) You will create a galley/ARC or review copy of the book, send it to book industry and long-lead reviewers (e.g., magazines, newspapers, etc.), and notify libraries and bookstores about your book. These are just a small sample of marketing ideas. You will also pitch yourself for interviews to radio, TV, blogs, and podcasts and do those interviews. You will also promote yourself on social media (Facebook, Instagram, Pinterest, Twitter, Threads, Goodreads, LinkedIn, etc.)

Good News: The profits from the sale of your books is 100% your profit, the rights to the book are yours, the control of the content is yours. Options: you can choose to publish an eBook alone, to print-on-demand versus printing a run of thousands of books, or any variation of the two. You may also wish to work with a distributor, aggregator, or retailer who will help you with sales and fulfillment for a piece of your profit, though not as much of a piece as if you went with a traditional publisher! More on this in the "Variations of Self-Publishing" section.

> When you self-publish, you create your own mini-business to publish your first author's book!

Bad news: You must create/pay for the interior design, the book cover design, the galleys/ARCs, the eBook file creation, the index (if there is one), the ISBN numbers, the CIP (Cataloging in Publication) data, and the printing of the books (if you choose to print). The fulfillment of sales is your responsibility, as is all the promotion and publicity, plus the financial reporting required for your new publishing business.

As you can see from the *Self-Publishing Flowchart*, you do all of the tasks (or delegate them). You wear two hats, that of author and that of publisher. It may seem daunting, but establishing yourself as a publisher first, and then as an author, may be the right choice for you.

VARIATIONS ON SELF-PUBLISHING

There are alternative ways to self-publishing. What we described above was the "traditional" way to self-publish that gave you the basics of how the process works. There are alternatives. As of this writing, there are self-publishing businesses that offer ways to get your book published quickly as an eBook or by Print-On-Demand. Some offer services to distribute your book when completed and others offer services to help you complete the book (interior design, eBook file creation, etc.) as well as to distribute your book to various online platforms. Each self-publishing business must be investigated thoroughly to make sure it fits your needs and goals.

WARNING: Many distribution platforms, Amazon KDP, for example, come with contracts of exclusivity. This means that your book will only be available for sale in one place for a period of time. Some platforms allow book sales in many places, but not others. Your book may be limited in review opportunities and distribution opportunities in bookstores, libraries and international outlets. If you are not offering a physical book option, there may also be limits on where you can sell or be reviewed. A few examples of these limited self-publishing retail/aggregator companies are AmazonKDP, Draft2Digital, and Book Baby.

Hybrid Publishing is similar to traditional publishing with one major exception. If you sign with a hybrid publisher to publish your book you will be contributing money toward the creation and publication of the book. The hybrid publisher will also contribute money and be responsible for the production and distribution of the book. Because the author will be paying upfront for services, the author will also receive a higher royalty than they would from a traditional publisher.

Every hybrid publisher is different and each contract is unique. There have been reports of authors who absolutely love their hybrid publishers. These authors simply don't have the time or desire to learn the ins and outs of publishing in order to self-publish and have no problem paying for that crucial guidance.

We suggest that you vet any hybrid publishing company that you are considering and review their client/author experiences before making a decision to work with them. The critically important question to ask when signing a contract with a hybrid publisher is, "Who owns the rights to the book, the publisher or the author?" If the answer is the publisher, then it is a vanity publisher, not a legitimate hybrid publisher. A traditional publisher will buy the rights from you, not just take them.

Finally, we briefly touched on many of the tasks of traditional publishers and self-publishers, but by no means have we provided a complete how-to. This was intentional. Google "self-publishing" to find many resources available to comprehensively help you in the step-by-step process. We do, however, have some broad-stroke ideas to point you in the right direction for each decision.

OUR BROAD STROKES ON THE TRADITIONAL PUBLISHING ROUTE AND THE SELF-PUBLISHING ROUTE

YOUR FIRST STEP TO PUBLISH YOUR BOOK: TRADITIONAL PUBLISHING

No matter which publishing path you choose, you start by actually writing the book. Get it all down in a Word document. Well, duh ... you might be thinking ... writing is the obvious first step to publishing a book. You would be surprised by how many aspiring authors simply have an **idea** for a book and feel that the idea is enough to pitch to a publisher. Trust us, an idea is not enough. Writing the book, or most of the book, is the first step. Completing the book will prove that you have the fortitude and enough material to write a full-length book!

After you write the book, or most of the book, you have a manuscript! Yes, a manuscript. It is very exciting. The next step is to come up with a query. A query is a one page "pitch" or summary of your book and of you. In Part Two there are exercises designed to help you identify **your audience, your message, and your hook** for your book. **Audience, message, and hook** decisions will be useful in creating a query. (See *Your Book Marketing Essentials* on page 36 for more information.) There are many examples of a good query letter online. The most important tip for writing a query is to read the instructions for submissions on the website of the agent or publisher you want to query. Follow their instructions to the letter. If you are approaching multiple agents and/or publishers, make sure each query is tailored specifically to the person you are contacting.

Armed with your manuscript and your query, you can start your journey to find a publisher.

PITCHING TO A TRADITIONAL PUBLISHER OR AGENT

Most top publishers will **only** accept a book submission from an agent. They will not accept a book submission directly from an author. If you are looking at the top publishing companies to publish your book, your first step is to find an agent who will represent you. There are, however, many publishers that DO accept "unsolicited" book submissions and they will clearly state that on their website.

> Search for "author submission" or "submissions" on a publisher and agent website. You will find their unique instructions there.

The pitching process for agents and publishers is essentially the same. They will both have submission instructions on their websites to direct you on how to pitch to them. READ their submission instructions and exactly FOLLOW their submission instructions. If you send a submission that does NOT follow their instructions, it provides an easy decision for them to say no to you.

For most agents and publishers, their first look at your pitch is the query, which is why we suggest that you start by writing one. Again, the query should be well-written, spell-checked, and compelling. Include the best stuff about your book in the first paragraph; it might be the only paragraph that gets read. Include a current, fascinating statistic and/or your **hook** in those first lines. Your goal is for the publisher or agent to understand that there is a need for this book and that you are the one to provide it!

HOW DO YOU FIND PUBLISHERS OR AGENTS TO PITCH?

We will share a few of our ideas here, but you should know that there are many resources where agents and publishers are listed, for example, books and online indexes like *Writers Digest* and *Literary Marketplace* for example.

Here are a few do-it-yourself ideas that we have tried and have found success.

First, purchase a spiral notebook. Write only on the right side of each page. Do not write on the back of any page. Use the right side of the page to document the names of agents and publishers that you select to send your query. When you pitch to them, record the date. Also record their responses as they come in. The last thing you want to do is pitch a query to an agent or publisher more than once! A notebook will document your outreach and prevent a duplicate pitch.

To find agents and publishers, hop on the "Google machine" and start searching. We promise that although the work may seem tedious (we know it was hard work just to write the book) your research will pay off, not only in the form of actual information, but also in the skill you will develop to quickly find information on any website you search. Book marketing requires a great deal of research!

Here's our favorite tip to identify a possible agent or publisher. Let's say you wrote a book of ghost stories. Ghost stories are your favorite and you own many such books. Crack open those books and look through the first few pages. Identify the publisher of the books. Perhaps the publisher would also like to publish YOUR book. Read the acknowledgements page. Did the author thank an agent? Perhaps that agent would like to represent YOU. Are there pages of endorsements or "praise blurbs" from other authors? Are those other author's books about ghosts, too? Who published THEIR books? Who were their agents?

You get the idea. Research each possible publisher and agent online. If they are a good fit, send them a query or pitch.

I am sure it has occurred to you that Amazon would be a great place to try the technique described above. You would be correct. Goodreads and Library Thing are also great resources to search books by genre and identify agents and publishers.

For most publishers and agents, you can go to their websites and find the page that lists "author submission" or "submissions." You will rapidly determine if a publisher accepts a submission directly from you or if you have to go through an agent. On an agent's webpage, you will swiftly find instructions for "submissions."

OUR BROAD STROKES ON THE SELF-PUBLISHING ROUTE

Once again, the first step in getting your book published is to actually write the book. Get it all down in a Word document. You now have a manuscript.

We mentioned in the **Introduction** that there are many ways to self-publish. What is common to self-publishing options is the fact that if you want your book to be professionally produced, you will need to hire some help, no matter what version of self-publishing you select.

THE MOST IMPORTANT DECISION YOU WILL MAKE AS A SELF-PUBLISHER? THE PEOPLE YOU HIRE!

The first, and perhaps most important tip is to spend the money to hire an editor. You simply cannot do it yourself. Spend the money on a reputable editor. You will not be sorry.

Next, let's say you have decided to release your book as a print-on-demand book (no inventory) and an eBook. Unless you have the necessary software and design skills, you will need to hire a book designer to create the interior layout for a printed version. The layout files have very specific dimensions for print-on-demand, and sometimes different ones for a traditional printer. An eBook file must also be created. A proper eBook file has very specific dimensions to be accepted on the different eBook platforms. You will also need a book cover designer. Book covers matter! If your book cover is amateurish, you will lose sales and reviewers. Book cover files also have specific requirements for print and eBook. MS Word is a great program to use when you're writing your manuscript, but it will not suffice for the design/layout of your book. You get the idea.

Our most important tip is to vet anyone you select to hire to handle these most valuable tasks in book creation. Make sure you hire an editor who has experience editing ... not just someone who reads all the time. Make sure that the designer you select has created files for a print book and an eBook and knows the book industry requirements. Ask to see their previous work. Ask for author or publishing references and then check them out. Do not use your cousin Bill to do this work, unless Bill is a professional book designer!

When Claudine published her first book, she hired an editor. She hired an indexer. She hired a firm to create her book layout and book cover. She hired a book printer. Finally, she hired a book marketer on an hourly basis. She did much of the marketing herself, but used the book marketer to guide her thorough the process and act as her publicist contact. Her book marketer helped her find a distributor. She received 1,500 books at her home from her printer. She sent 1,500 books to her distributor. She did her own marketing, publicity and fulfillment of the orders of her book. Everything was completed within a reasonable budget. It can be done. The lesson is that she took the time to hire the right people! Take the time to hire reputable people.

BOOK DISTRIBUTION OPTIONS FOR THE SELF-PUBLISHED AND TRADITIONALLY PUBLISHED

Book distribution is important to understand for both traditionally published (published with a formal publisher like Simon & Schuster) and self-published authors. To review, let's take a step back from distribution and review publishing choices and then how distribution plays a role in getting your book seen and sold. You have 3 publishing choices:

1. Traditional Publishing 2. Self-Publishing 3. Hybrid Publishing

Traditional publishing: the publishing company (i.e., Sourcebooks) handles everything to create your book. They then distribute it and sell it. The **publisher** has the sole rights to publish, market and distribute the book as they deem appropriate. You, the author, provide the manuscript and support the book marketing.

Self-publishing: You create your book, distribute it and sell it. **You own your book.** You could create a formal publishing company yourself (as a business) and THEN publish your own book in a traditional manner. Claudine created a publishing company, for example, and called it New Buck Press. In 2008, New Buck Press purchased ISBN numbers, hired an editor and a book designer, secured a distribution contract, printed and then fulfilled orders for her first book, *It Gets Easier and Other Lies We Tell New Mothers*.

On the other hand, it is not necessary to create your own publishing company. You can create your book from a Word doc, upload it to a retailer (like KDP), and be "published." However, if you want to get your book seen and sold you need a balance between creating your own publishing company and simply uploading a word document to a retailer (or aggregator). A shrewd book distribution strategy, as well as a professionally packaged book, is key for successful self-publishing.

Hybrid Publishing is a combination of Traditional Publishing and Self-Publishing. The author financially contributes to the making of the book and the publisher takes on some of the traditional roles of publishing. If you are considering a hybrid publisher, before you sign a contract, make sure you have an explicit understanding of what they are going to provide in exchange for what you are providing (book and financial). It is important to understand all of the pieces of any contract you enter into, whether it be with a hybrid or traditional publisher. If they are not clear to you, engage the services of an attorney who has some experience with publishing contracts.

It is a good option for people who want to write a book and don't have the time to promote it as much as others. If this route is chosen, make sure to determine who owns the rights to the book. That's part of the negotiation, unless the hybrid publisher has set guidelines for that.

WHAT IS BOOK DISTRIBUTION AND WHY IS IT IMPORTANT?

An easy way to understand book distribution is to compare it to the cable TV shows. A show that starts on one cable channel can also end up on other paid platform channels. For example, the STARZ show *Outlander* can also be seen on Netflix and Amazon Prime Video. The owner of the show distributes the show to several video platforms. Each platform pays for the show. Book distribution works in a similar fashion. Your book can be uploaded to many different platforms (retailers and aggregators) who then sell the book on their platforms. Movies that you see in the theater are another example. When you watch a movie, the beginning credits flash company names introduced with the phrase "brought to you by." Many of those companies are movie distributors.

As a self-publisher, **you** decide on the distribution strategy for your book. You can mix and match distribution platforms to sell your book as well. To understand your book distribution choices, you first need to know the difference between **book retailer** and **book aggregator**. Both can be used to distribute books.

Get Your Book Seen and Sold

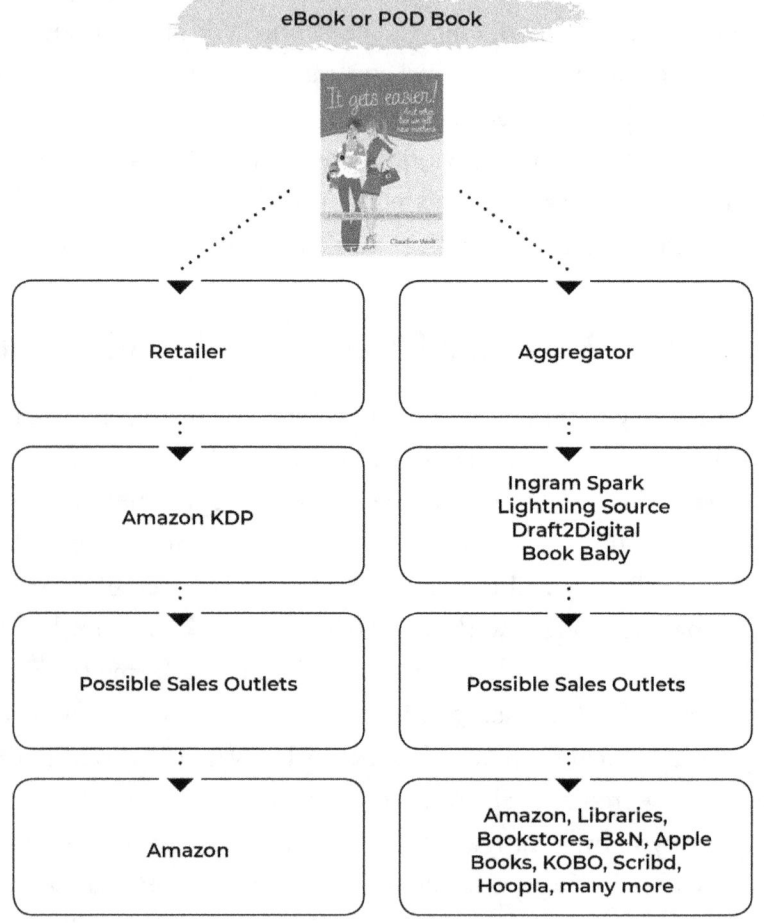

BOOK DISTRIBUTION CHOICES – RETAILERS vs AGGREGATORS

BOOK RETAILERS

A book retailer takes your already created book file and offers it for sale on their site. You upload your eBook and/or print-on-demand (POD) file to their website (following their directions, of course) and they list it for sale on their website. They take a cut of the sale. Amazon (KDP) is a great example and it just happens to have the biggest slice of the market as a book seller. Because they have millions of books for sale, Amazon can make it difficult for new books to be seen. If you select **Amazon's KDP Select Program,** Amazon is the only place you can sell it for a period of time.

NOTE: You CAN select Amazon to distribute your eBook and opt out of the KDP Select program. If you opt out, they do NOT have exclusivity and you can then place your book with other distributors as well. (More on this to follow.)

BOOK AGGREGATORS

So what is an aggregator? The aggregator is the middleman between you and the retailer. An aggregator is a company that takes your book and gets it placed on different online platforms (Kobo, Apple Books), retailers (Amazon and Barnes & Noble) as well as bookstores and libraries in some cases. You will need to find out which aggregators work with which platforms and retailers and which distribute eBooks and/or print books so that you reach the target audience that is right for your book.

Each book aggregator is a little different so they each must be researched to see if there is a good fit for you. You can also work with several aggregators. Once you submit your book (eBook & POD) to them, they will submit your book to the other sales platforms for you.

MIX AND MATCH AGGREGATORS
A DISTRIBUTION STRATEGY

There are several ways to sell through Amazon and other retailers. You can also mix and match aggregators as a distribution strategy with one exception noted below.

For example, for your print book you could use IngramSpark, which would then print and distribute your book on many platforms including Amazon, Barnes & Noble (B&N), other bookstores, and libraries. IngramSpark has a great reputation for quality print-on-demand books.

For your eBook, you could use Draft2Digital. They will take your completed eBook and submit it to many other platforms online: Amazon, Apple Books, B&N, Kobo, Scribd, Hoopla, and libraries.

You could also distribute to individual retailers and other online platforms and not use an aggregator at all if you were so inclined and had the time to manage it! However, keep in mind that if you decide to take this route, you will need to have adequate storage space for your books and the time necessary to process and ship orders to buyers.

WE KNOW, WE KNOW – AMAZON KINDLE DIRECT PUBLISHING (KDP)

Many authors use Amazon KDP to sell their eBooks. Amazon is not an aggregator. It is a retailer. You upload your finished eBook through Amazon's KDP program and they sell your eBook for you on Amazon. KDP is a popular distribution choice for some authors because Amazon has such a huge percentage of the book buying market. The idea behind selecting KDP is the hope that your book would have the best chance to be seen and sold.

Your Publishing Choices

However, keep in mind that Amazon is a very crowded bookshop. Some other platforms with less competition might give your book a better chance to be seen. There are many other online platforms: Apple Books, KOBO Writing Life, iBooks, and others. **That being said, don't neglect Amazon. It doesn't cost extra to place your book there, and if someone is looking specifically for your book, that is probably the first place they'll go.**

DISTRIBUTION OPTIONS FOR YOUR EBOOK USING AMAZON KDP

Another distribution option could be to go to Amazon KDP directly and upload your eBook for sale and also sign up with an aggregator like Draft2Digital, which will place your book on many other platforms.

Book distribution retailers and aggregators are changing all the time. They add services, change offerings, deals, conditions, and sometimes they even merge. Look at these choices as more options for you to get your books seen and sold!

> KDP SELECT is a separate Amazon program. You upload your eBook and promise EXCLUSIVITY with Amazon, meaning that you promise NOT to sell your eBook anywhere else for a period of time, at least 90 days. That would mean no aggregators for your eBook if you select the KDP SELECT program. Again, you do not have to pick the KDP Select program for your eBook. You could opt out of that and sign up for the regular KDP program.

WHY DO I NEED TO CARE ABOUT DISTRIBUTION IF I AM TRADITIONALLY PUBLISHED?

You already know that regardless of whether you are self-published or traditionally published you need to market your book. The same responsibility applies to the distribution of your book. Yes, your publisher will handle distribution, but wouldn't it be useful to know their distribution strategy as well? If you are informed about it, you can ask questions and make suggestions. At the very least, you can use the information to monitor your book's success.

WE GOT IN THE WEEDS A BIT

This guide is NOT a detailed publishing "how-to". However, book distribution is SUCH an important topic. It is critical for you to understand how distribution works when making your decisions. The time you spend researching your options will make the choices more understandable. You may even find yourself excited about the number of options and ways to get your book seen and sold. Remember, there is more than ONE way to distribute your book, whether traditionally published or self-published.

Now that we've covered the different ways you can publish, it is time to discuss book marketing and promotion!

PART TWO

Marketing and Promotion

GET YOUR BOOK SEEN AND SOLD

Book Marketing Overview

The breadth of a possible book marketing strategy

Identify the Goal for Your Book
↓
Message | Audience | Hook
↓
Book Distribution Plan
↓
Develop Media Kit Items
(press release, author bio, book sell sheet, Q&A, etc)
↓
Pre-Publication Book Review Outreach
↙ ↘
Book Industry Reviewers   Endorsements & Other Reviews
↓
Create Media Contacts List
↙ ↓ ↓ ↓ ↘
Magazine   Newspaper   Podcast   Website   Radio
↓
Pitch Pre-Publication Media
↓
Launch Day Events
↙ ↓ ↘
Book Signing   F/B Live.   Instagram Live
↓
Keep Going
↙ ↓ ↘
Pitch to Media   Gather Reviews   Post on Social Media

HAVE FUN!

INTRODUCTION

After reading Part One, you may have decided HOW you want to publish your book. You might be pitching to traditional publishers and/or agents OR you are starting your own publishing company. Well done!

Now comes the fun part — the marketing and promotion of your book to get it seen and sold!

Before we dive into the workbook exercises, we want to share something with you about marketing.

FEAR OF MARKETING: WE GET IT

There is nothing that strikes fear into the heart of an author more than the words "you need to promote yourself." We get it. No one likes to run around asking people to buy their book or to talk about how great they are. It makes us uncomfortable. We all know that

> You are not selling something. You are sharing what your audience already desires.

salesperson who traps us with a "hard-sell pitch." The hard sell starts casually enough. The person talks about how great their product is and, at first, it is fine to listen. Next, inevitably, comes the discomfort. The salesperson says, "What do you think?" "Would you like to buy my product?" You may timidly offer various versions of a "no" answer. (Or "Not right now," "I'll think about it," or "I don't have the money.") The salesperson will simply not take no for an answer. Close, close, close — ABC — Always Be Closing. The salesman gives more reasons why you simply HAVE to HAVE what they are selling. More discomfort. They send you texts, emails, newsletters. They may even call you! The hard sell. This is NOT what we mean by marketing and publicizing your new book. Take heart.

WHAT KIND OF PROMOTION ARE WE TALKING ABOUT?

We are talking about putting your message out there, not selling yourself. Your message? The message in your book is something the world needs. It is something the world wants. Once the book is out there and people know about it, there is no hard sell. Readers will buy because they need the message. The selling takes care of itself. Do not worry. You are not selling something. You are sharing what your audience already desires. No stress. The work is getting the word out about the message. The work you do before the book is actually published is a critical element to selling it once it is published. The preparation will be fun and productive!

MESSAGE, AUDIENCE, HOOK

First, we need to discuss and nail down three important things: **Message, Audience, Hook.** Decisions about these three things lead to the creation of great marketing tools and a solid and effective Marketing Plan!

MARKETING TOOLS – GET YOUR BOOK SEEN AND SOLD

In the next section, we will share the **marketing tools** you need to carry out your marketing tasks.

Quick example: Let's say your **Marketing Plan** includes a pitch to a local radio station to interview you. Great Idea! What marketing tools, for example, do you need to pitch to a local radio station?

> **Radio Show Contact Information:**
> Name, Email, Phone (Part of your Media Contact List)
> **Pitch**
> **Press Release**
> **Author Bio**

We will review many marketing tools and teach you how to create them in this section.

Marketing and Promotion

MARKETING PLAN – GET YOUR BOOK SEEN AND SOLD

We are also going to describe a basic plan to market, promote, and sell your book with an example from the Marketing Plan for Claudine's first book. Plus, we will share THE SECRET . . . the most important part of your Marketing Plan.

Are you excited to get started? Let's begin!

YOUR BOOK MARKETING ESSENTIALS

MESSAGE, AUDIENCE, HOOK – OH MY

We previously mentioned that you need a **Marketing Plan** and **marketing tools** to get your book seen and sold. There are three items that you need to nail down BEFORE you can even begin to create a Marketing Plan and those marketing tools. They are MESSAGE, AUDIENCE, and HOOK.

The good news is that all the work you will do in the next few pages will be used in every marketing tool you create and in your Marketing Plan. This work will help you focus, strategize, and create all of your future marketing to get your book seen and sold. Here are some quickie definitions and then . . . **Let's Do It!**

Message, Audience, Hook — Oh My!

MESSAGE

What message do you need to share with your book? Most simply, what do you want your readers to learn from you? If this makes you panic, go right to the next page.

AUDIENCE

Who are your specific book buyers? We do not mean the readers who **may possibly** buy your book, but the **specific** group of readers who **will** buy your book— the readers you had in mind when you wrote this book. Don't worry; we have a fantastic exercise to help you nail down your targeted readers.

HOOK

A "hook" is a scintillating aspect of your book, or YOU, or YOUR STORY, that is so compelling and unique that others will WANT to tell your story.

*****

Now that we have the definitions down for these most important book marketing vocabulary terms, let's start to nail down the details of each for YOUR book.

> Identifying the message, the audience, and the hook of your book will help you focus, strategize, and create all of your future marketing and promotion to get your book seen and sold.

NOTE: Whether you choose a traditional publisher or a self-publisher, clearly identifying your message, audience, and hook will be invaluable to the success of your book.

YOUR MESSAGE
YOU ARE SHARING WHAT YOUR AUDIENCE ALREADY DESIRES

Always remember that you are sharing a message that your audience already desires. You are not selling anything. The process of identifying your message is fun because **you** know your message better than anyone. You care about your message more than anyone. You needed to share your message so badly that you wrote a book! YOU are the person who will come up with the best ideas for sharing your message. YOU will know who and where to pitch your story. YOU are the one who cares the most, so you will be the one who will work the hardest. Once you start to get responses to your marketing and promotion efforts, you will love it and have fun. More ideas will flow. You will be on a roll, and there is nothing more fun than seeing your message out in the world.

Here are two exercises to help you identify your message(s).

MESSAGE EXERCISE #1 (WITH AN EXAMPLE – BRAIN DUMP)

We will share a few books that we published or marketed and the messages of each. Claudine's first book had a bunch of messages: Honesty in Motherhood, Honesty in Parenting, Humor in Motherhood, Tips for Baby, Tips for New Moms, Relationship Changes with a New Baby, Working Mom Issues, Stay at Home Mom Issues, Judgement in Motherhood, New Baby Sleep Tips, New Mom Healing Tips, Sleep Schedule, Babysitters for Newborns, Maslow's Hierarchy of Needs, Fulfillment, and Breastfeeding.

The first step in distilling a message is to simply **brain dump** all the messages you are trying to share. Have a look at the brain dump example using the messages above. Simply use the example and the blank "brain dump" workbook page to write all the possible messages that you want to share with **your audience**. Dump it all out of your

Message, Audience, Hook — Oh My!

---

brain. You need to see it all out in one place. Messages may be used or they may not be used. Again, simply dump it all out of your brain and onto the paper. Below is how this example of a Brain Dump Message exercise from my first book would look on paper.

MESSAGE, AUDIENCE, HOOK... OH MY!

Brain Dump Exercise – Message

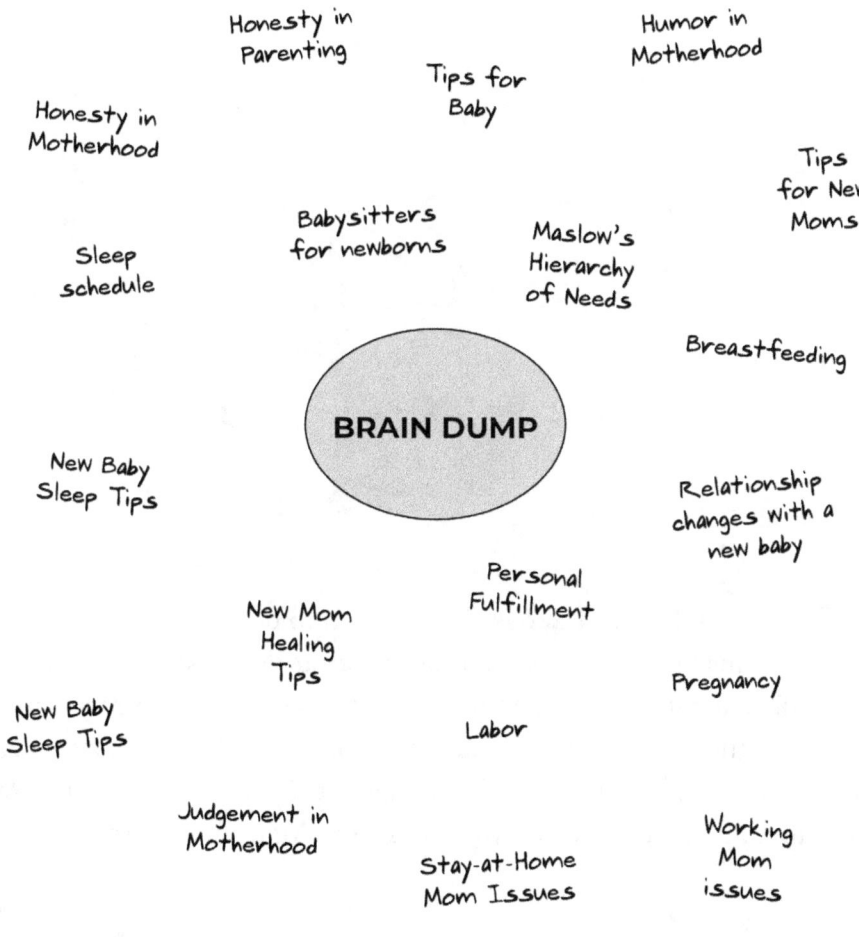

Now it's your turn. Fill out your **Message Brain Dump Exercise Worksheet.**

MESSAGE, AUDIENCE, HOOK... OH MY!

Brain Dump Exercise – Message

That **Brain Dump Exercise** is super fun to do, right?

In the next exercise, answer a few penetrating questions to get even more juice flowing about your message. Take some time to process these questions thoughtfully and write down your answers. The answers can be used in many Media Kit tools and marketing ideas, but right now we want to help you to focus on your most important messages.

MESSAGE EXERCISE #2

Dig in deep here. Take some time to think about your message and where it might lead.

Does your book solve a problem?

Why is your book important to share?

How will your book impact the reader? How will your book make the reader feel?

Will your book help the reader's life? In what way?

Why is sharing your message so important to you and/or to the world?

Why are you uniquely qualified to share the information in your book?

Take a few minutes and identify the three most important messages you wish to convey with your book and then write them down.

DISTILLING AN OVERALL MESSAGE

Now that you have uncovered all the possible messages that you want to share, you need to pinpoint the most important message — the overall message. All of the messages in your brain dump exercise and the answered questions can be used in your marketing tools, but for now we want you to arrive at an overall message . . . a message that can be used in your Elevator Pitch. What's an Elevator Pitch?

THE ELEVATOR PITCH

For *It Gets Easier and Other Lies We Tell New Mothers* our brain dump session was productive, with many possible messages that we could use in different ways. However, a decision on an **overall message** was important.

Why? One overall message will be needed for your Elevator Pitch — the heart of your press release and other marketing tools. What is an Elevator Pitch? An Elevator Pitch is exactly what it sounds like: a pitch that you would make to someone you meet in an elevator — a quick, pithy sentence or two that will let a stranger know exactly what your book is about. To illustrate, imagine being in the elevator with a stranger.

The stranger asks: "What do you do?"

You answer: "I'm an author."

Stranger: "Cool, what's your book about?"

You: "Well, it's a book for parents that helps with a baby or a newborn baby that's kind of funny but is also helpful with new mom issues and has tips and helps to get your baby to sleep through the night but also helps moms with becoming a new mom."

Stranger: [silence]

Message, Audience, Hook — Oh My!

Why is the stranger silent? Because the stranger exited the elevator! You took too long to describe your book and she has no idea if she would be interested in purchasing it.

Now imagine responding with the Elevator Pitch you created in advance by pulling from your brain dump and message exercises.

Let's try that Elevator Pitch Example again:

Stranger asks: "Cool; what is your book about?"

You: "It's a fun, practical guide for new moms!"

Stranger: "Awesome. I need that book. I'll buy it as soon as I get home!"

Do you see the difference? A run-on sentence vs. a six-word pitch? Our Elevator Pitch for *Get Your Book Seen and Sold* is:

A fun, easy guide for writers who want to publish and market a book.

This Elevator Pitch uses **the most powerful words** you used in the previous exercises to express the meaning of the book. Look at the words we selected in our pitch.

Fun: powerful word, right? The word "fun" conveys lightheartedness, an activity that the reader will enjoy, a non-threatening activity.

Easy: sometimes fun is not exactly easy. We want to convey easy. Come join us in this activity. It's okay. You can do this.

Guide: with one word, we convey that this book will be interactive, that you will walk away with something concrete, a plan. We convey that you can write in this book. We convey that this book will become a resource for you. We convey a sense of potential accomplishment. The reader knows that once they do the exercises in the guide, they have accomplished something — a great feeling. Wow! Pretty powerful word!

Writers: We are specific about who we are helping. Again, non-threatening. We are your fellow writers and we are here to share our knowledge because that is what colleagues do — we help each other.

A few more examples of Elevator Pitches that we created:

For a book we marketed, called *Televenge*, we had this Elevator Pitch:

A suspense thriller

For another book we marketed, titled *Super Baby Food*, we came up with this Elevator Pitch:

Easy, homemade, organic baby food

Are you getting the idea? To create your Elevator Pitch, take some time to analyze your answers to the questions in the exercises above. Identify the most powerful words to describe your book. It might also be advantageous to talk through your ideas for an Elevator Pitch with a friend. This could help you keep it simple and identify the most powerful words.

Write several possible Elevator Pitches (five or six words each).

Pick the most pithy and powerful Elevator Pitch and write it here.

Look at how much you are getting done, you book marketer, you! You already have a bunch of messages and an overall message fashioned as your Elevator Pitch. Well done!

The next step is to identify your audience.

> An Elevator Pitch is exactly what it sounds like. A pitch that you would give to someone you meet in an elevator — a quick, pithy sentence that will let a stranger know exactly what your book is about.

YOUR AUDIENCE:
WHO WILL BUY YOUR BOOK?

Here is where you get very specific about who will buy your book.

Why do you need to get specific? You need to get specific about your book buyers because you need to know where to focus your marketing efforts. You need to go where your audience will see your book. This is going to be so much fun; trust us!

AUDIENCE EXERCISE

Close your eyes for a minute. Take three breaths. Inhale slowly and completely. Exhale slowly and completely. Now, imagine a book buyer picking your book off the shelf of a bookstore or library. Don't rush the image. Consider this exercise a meditation. Once you are nice and relaxed, answer some questions about the reader you imagined.

How old is your reader?

Any children?

Is your reader married?

What is your reader's gender?

What are your reader's interests?

Does your reader work outside the home?

Does your reader homeschool?

Can you name some common life occurrences of your reader and other potential readers?

Where does your reader shop?

When does your reader shop? What day of the week? What time of day?

Where does your reader live?

How does your reader dress?

Where does your reader eat?

What does your reader eat?

What does your reader do in his/her free time?

What other books, and what kind of books, interest your reader?

What are your readers' professions?

Do they volunteer? If so, where?

Do they belong to clubs? What are they?

What shows do they watch?

What magazines do they read?

Do they read the newspaper?

What subjects interest them?

What do they talk about with their friends, family or co-workers?

Are they on social media?

What social media do they like the best? Why do they like it the best?

Do they listen to podcasts? Which podcasts? Why do they focus on those podcasts?

Do they listen to the radio? Local? National? NPR? All three?

With the answers to these questions, you can develop a book buyer profile analysis that will help you identify your audience and where to find them. If you know where to find your audience, you will know where to focus your book marketing efforts. Make sense?

Here is an example of a book buyer profile analysis for my next book, *Stories and Strategies for Women*.

Who will by this book?

Women, working or stay-at-home mothers, married or newly separated, 35 to 55 years old, household income over $75,000, will purchase this book. They are well-dressed, stylish, and live in the suburbs. They read, play tennis, go to parks, attend kid's sporting events, exercise and do yoga. They own Pelotons and/or treadmills. They work part-time from home, have transitioned in their career to an entrepreneurial business, or are doing full-time corporate work.

They are community-minded and join the YMCA, Cornerstone Gym, or Orangetheory Fitness, or at least they did before COVID. They volunteer at local non-profit organizations.

They are talking to their friends about work-life balance, motherhood/parenting, marriage and relationships. They join book clubs to discuss a book, yes, but also to catch up with friends. They still go to the library.

They binge-watch *Big Little Lies*, *Little Fires Everywhere*, *The Phantom Prince* documentary, *Mindhunter*, *Mad Men*, *Ozark*, *Schitt's Creek*, *Dead to Me*, and *Killing Eve*. What do these shows have in common? That's easy. They all feature strong women in positions of challenge and/or turmoil who keep fighting for their best life. Many of the programs are written and produced by women, and women are ravenously consuming them and sharing their good fortune with other potential viewers. These viewers sip wine and share their fears with their friends. They are not afraid to be vulnerable and are strong enough to make changes to be happy. They call out what is not working in their lives and they take steps to change it. They fight against convention. At the same time, they embrace romance with a partner and closer relationships with their kids. They do not shy away from sentiment.

They shop and buy online at Amazon after searching for non-fiction bestsellers that they have researched by topic. They buy self-help books and books about health, diet, and beauty. They listen to Audible Books while they commute to work or drive the kids to their activities. They check Goodreads for reviews and will buy on Barnes & Noble. They see books that grab their attention in the specialty section of Anthropologie. They listen to recommendations from their friends. They buy cookbooks (Pioneer Woman, Rachel Ray, Gina Homolka, *Skinny Taste*).

They purchase on Mondays, when they are back to work, after thinking about their issues over the weekend or experiencing an issue

Message, Audience, Hook — Oh My!

over the weekend. They buy in the afternoons when their children nap. They buy on Sunday evening when they have a minute of peace.

They listen to talk radio, NPR and local radio stations, to find out what is going on locally in their communities, like my station, WDVR, in Sergeantsville, New Jersey, where Claudine hosts and produces a weekly talk show, *Let's Talk!* They listen to podcasts about true crime (for escape) "Cold," "Dirty John," "The Teacher's Pet," "Real Crime Profile," "My Favorite Murder," podcasts of successful women (for tips) such as "Secrets of Wealthy Women WSJ," and podcasts that tell stories (for fun and personal growth) like "Office Ladies," "Lore," "You Must Remember This," and Claudine's podcast, "Stories and Strategies for Women."

You can see from this audience analysis that you can get very specific and creative. Have fun with this exercise and let your mind run free. You will return to this tool that you have created again and again to identify possible markets to sell your book and possible ways to market your book. Well done!

> A book-buyer profile analysis will help you to identify your audience and where to find them. If you know where to find your audience, you will know where to focus your book marketing efforts to sell to them.

A SPECIFIC EXAMPLE OF NARROWING A TARGET AUDIENCE

When Claudine was in the process of self-publishing *It Gets Easier and Other Lies We Tell New Mothers*, she needed to identify her **specific target audience**. She had some trouble, so she got on the phone with a friend who owned her own retail business and was a whiz at marketing. She spent 20 minutes on the phone with Claudine and they hashed it out. Identifying a specific, target audience was revolutionary for her to be able to market her book. Because she had narrowed her target audience, she was able to strategically name her website, her Twitter handle and all her social media. We determined a specific target audience with a role-play exercise.

Who will read this book?
All women

Get specific; what group will overwhelmingly read this book?
Mothers

What kind of mothers? Pregnant mothers, first time mothers, older mothers, grandmothers?
Mothers of a first-born or subsequently born baby

Pick one, not both
Mothers of a first-born baby

So a NEW MOM
Yes, A New Mom!

That was her audience — New Moms. You can see where the bubble of "All Women" was too big. Yes, pregnant moms might like the book, but would they really benefit from the book? Primarily, the information in the book was for the first-time New Mom — a woman who had her baby and was ready for practical, honest tips with a sense of humor. Others may buy the book and that is great, but the specific, target audience for the book was the New Mom!

Claudine took the step to discover where new moms hang out online and in the community and focused her marketing there. She named her website help4newmoms.com and set her Twitter handle as @help4newmoms. See what a revelation identifying a target audience is? She researched where "new mom" stories are published (magazines,

Message, Audience, Hook — Oh My!

newspapers) and where on the radio "new moms" stories are aired and focused her marketing in those places. She researched new mom clubs, new mom trade shows, new mom blogs. Once she had her target market identified, many marketing tools and efforts fell right into place.

We suggest that you find a friend and work through the challenging questions to identify a specific target audience.

Do not fret about missing out on a different audience of book buyers. You can re-evaluate as your book marketing evolves to measure what works and what doesn't work. In Claudine's case, something interesting happened. *It Gets Easier and Other Lies We Tell New Mothers* has become a favorite baby shower gift! Who would have thought? A gift book! It turns out that the title of the book gets a laugh out loud when opened in a baby shower venue. Experienced moms smile and nod at the truth of it and the practical advice can be enjoyed by the new mom when she is ready in the months ahead. You simply never know all the audiences who will embrace your book!

You are on your way to identifying your book's audience. Now it's time to come up with your book's hook.

HOOK, HOOK, MY LIFE FOR A HOOK

So far, we have helped you to identify the messages you want to share with your book and to distill the most **important** message of your book (to keep your marketing focused) as well as an **Elevator Pitch** for you to share with potential buyers and whomever you meet. We also took you through an exercise to define a potential audience, as well as a specific target audience. Having identified your **message** and your **audience** will help in all of the marketing tools we will cover in the coming pages. The last ingredient we need to add to this recipe is for you to identify a **HOOK**.

WHAT IS A HOOK?

A hook is something about your book that distinguishes it from every other book of its kind out there. You have heard the phrase, "There is nothing new under the sun." So it is with a new book. Somewhere, somehow, there is another book out there that is like yours. You need to identify what makes YOUR book different. You need to come up with a reason for a literary agent or a publisher to take on your book if you decide to go the traditional book publishing route. You need a reason for a media contact — for example, your local radio show — to want to do an interview with you (publicity). You need a reason for distributors to want to sell your book to their clients (marketing). Once you decide on your hook, you will USE that hook in every marketing tool you produce. For example, you will use the hook in your press release, your pitches to media, your back-cover copy, your book's one-page sell sheet ... everywhere. If you have not secured a publisher yet, you will use it in your query and in your book proposal to traditional publishers and agents. Your hook is what will set you apart from all the other books out there.

A hook is something interesting, attention-grabbing, and/or different about your book or your story. A hook could also simply be about the author. For example, a celebrity author is a hook all by itself (think Michelle Obama). You may have more than one hook, too. You may be a celebrity who is writing a salacious story — hook and hook (Tina Turner's book about her life and her tumultuous relationship with Ike Turner).

Message, Audience, Hook — Oh My!

HOOK EXAMPLE

We worked with an author who wrote a fantastic book called *Super Baby Food*. The book was written 30 years ago and was well ahead of its time. In 1991, the author, Ruth Yaron, was writing about organic, homemade baby food and recipes to prepare it at home. In 1991!!! When we worked with Ms. Yaron, we were hired to help her with a 3rd edition of the book, to update it with her current recommendations and to create some marketing materials. We had three hooks.

One: "Famous super baby food book releases third edition." This was a hook because the original book was already famous. Readers were still buying the original in droves and were asking for a new edition.

Two: "Organic, homemade baby food." At the time that the third edition was released, organic, homemade baby food recipes were all the rage. Moms wanted to make their own baby food and needed direction. We took advantage of this existing demand. You may notice that this hook could also be considered an **Elevator Pitch** and a **message**! Sometimes a hook and an Elevator Pitch are the same.

Three: "Kourtney Kardashian reads *Super Baby Food*!" Kourtney Kardashian posted a picture of herself on Facebook reading the "popular purple book" after the birth of her first child. The Kardashians were very popular at the time. With that type of endorsement, we highlighted it for the new audience that we hoped to reach.

WHAT IS THE HOOK FOR AN UNKNOWN AUTHOR?

When Claudine self-published *It Gets Easier and Other Lies We Tell New Mothers*, there were other "girlfriend guide-type books" coming out and she was an unknown. How could she distinguish HER book? What was her hook? She focused on what made her book different... she highlighted honesty and humor in her book. Honesty and humor in motherhood is pretty common now, but way back in 2008, it was not so prevalent. It was almost as if humor and honesty were kept away from motherhood, as if motherhood was a secret, sacred institution that we must not breach. She wanted to blow that out of the water. She felt that if moms could start to speak honestly about motherhood with a sense of humor, it would bring mothers together and all the help that went along with it. So, one of her hooks was "honesty and humor in motherhood." A second hook, and another way to distinguish her book, was that she had lived and interviewed mothers on both sides of the country. She interviewed every mom she met. Distributors and the media found this an interesting aspect to her book and to her.

Sometimes a new hook can pop up after your book's release that can lead to a change in your marketing tools and lead to additional publicity opportunities. It is important to stay flexible. After Claudine released *It Gets Easier and Other Lies We Tell New Mothers,* one of her marketing pitches hit big. Early in the marketing process, she sent a galley of the book to author and nationally-syndicated radio personality, Dr. Laura Schlessinger. Dr. Laura loved the book, added it to her "Monday Picks" and *It Gets Easier and Other Lies We Tell New Mothers* was announced on her show as a giveaway to listeners. Because the radio show was nationally syndicated, millions heard about the book and it shot to #1 in the motherhood category on Amazon that day. Dr. Laura's approved blurb for the book: "This book is helpful and a hoot!" became another hook in marketing materials. (More on this story in **Media Contacts**.)

Another great example of a hook is something published in the Independent Book Publishers Association's January 2009 newsletter.

From: *"How Do I Find My Hook?"*

In explaining a hook, former producers of the *Oprah Winfrey Show*, Karen Melamed, Barbara Wellner, and LeGrande Green shared this example:

Message, Audience, Hook — Oh My!

A writer has a book of stories coming out about the haunted houses that line the East Coast. Well, that's nice. Heard it before. But one of the chapters is about a woman who met and fell in love with her ghost. Ok, now you got my attention.

Are you starting to understand what you need in a hook? It's something different and interesting. Something that a media contact can use to do a story. Something that is unique and motivating.

To determine **your** hook we start with . . . you guessed it . . . an exercise!

When we work with new authors who are interested in publishing and marketing their books, we ask them what their book is about and why they wrote it. You might feel some overlap with the Message exercise, but that's okay.

What is your book about?

Why did you write it?

Why are you the perfect person to write this book?

In an attempt to identify a hook, or hooks, the next thing we ask authors is a very powerful question. Before we share the question with you, however, we want to discuss an important aspect of book marketing.

Unless you are a celebrity, your hook is NEVER *"New Author Publishes Book."* Never Ever Ever. Guess why?

Because no one cares! We do not say this to be mean. It is simply a fact. People really don't care about you or your new book, unless of course you are J.K. Rowling or Harry Styles. People generally care about themselves and what your book can do for them.

We hate to be so negative, but this is a concept that you must understand. No one else cares that you wrote and published a book. Okay, maybe your mom and dad care. Perhaps even your spouse. That is about it. No one cares about YOU or your book.

What people care about is your message, your story, your hook. What the READER can get out of your book is key, not that fact that you wrote a book. The marketing tools that you create must reflect your message and what the reader can get out of your book. Will they glean unique knowledge? Will they gain new insight on something specific? Will their life be changed for the better after reading your book? Will they be entertained by reading your book? How will they be entertained? Why will they be entertained?

Ok, off the soap box. Back to the question we ask authors when we are trying to determine a hook for their book.

When working with authors, we ask the questions: **"Who cares? Why do they care?"**

In the example of *It Gets Easier and Other Lies We Tell New Mothers*, Claudine asked those questions of herself. Her answers:

> New moms will care. The book will provide new moms with honest information so that they will know that they are not alone in their frustration and joy. The book will provide practical tips for helping their baby sleep through the night so that they will sleep better, feel better, and be better equipped for the job of motherhood. This book will validate new moms' concerns

Message, Audience, Hook — Oh My!

and help them to understand that their feelings are normal. This book will be the girlfriend they may not have to assuage guilt and commiserate without feeling shame. This book will make new moms laugh and help them to not take life so seriously. This book will help them with gentle suggestions for relationships, finding babysitters, taking time for themselves, and encouraging her continuing quest for fulfillment. This book stresses the idea that moms are part of the family too and their needs must also be part of the family decision-making equation.

You will notice that nowhere in her answer did she say, "Claudine Wolk wrote a book." "Claudine Wolk wrote a book" is NOT the story! The story is the message of help for new moms.

Many times, we find the hook comes from the book itself and it simply takes a little digging to uncover it. For example, one author started her book with the history of her amazing grandmother. Her grandmother had emigrated to the United States in the early 1900s and was an entrepreneur. She made her own money and was sought after and respected in her community—quite a departure from most of the women of her time. Nana's clients included business leaders, police, and mafia leaders! Interesting, right? What a great hook. What a great story to pitch to potential magazines, newspapers, radio, and TV. We can see the headlines now.

"Lessons from Nana: A Female Entrepreneur Ahead of Her Time"
"Nana's Business Served Law Enforcement and Mafia Alike"
"My Nana Schmoozed with The Godfather and Turned a Pretty Profit, Too"

HOOK EXERCISE

Here is where you find your hook. Answer the questions below. After every answer (potential hook) answer the questions "Who cares?" and "Why do they care?" If you are having trouble, talk it through with a friend and ask them to hash it out with you.

What is unique about your book? (can be more than one thing)

Why will the reader care?

What is the most interesting thing that you write about in your book?

What will it do for the reader?

Do you introduce any new or unique concepts in your book?

Why will the reader care?

Message, Audience, Hook — Oh My!

Do you have some type of unique training or skill that you share in your book?

Why will the reader care?

Is there a popular overall theme to your book? Have you added a new twist to it?

Why will the reader care?

Well Done! You have done some serious work here. Congratulate yourself because the work you have just done will be integral in getting your book seen and sold!

With your message, audience, and hook identified you are ready to create your Marketing Tools!

MARKETING TOOLS: MEET THE MEDIA KIT

You have used the exercises in the previous pages to decide on your **Message, Audience and Hook.** Good work. Now it's time to apply that good work to create the marketing tools you will use to announce your book, build excitement for your book, and ultimately sell your book.

NOTE: If you decided to publish your book through a traditional publisher, many of the marketing tools we cover will be prepared and utilized by your publisher's publicity department. That's great. However, it is still a good idea to learn the purpose of the marketing tools and the details behind them. Additionally, your publisher will appreciate your contribution to creating these tools with the good work you have already done in the **Message, Audience, Hook, Oh My!** section. Remember, you know your book better than anyone! If you decided to self-publish, on the other hand, these tools will be invaluable to you and you will be the one creating them.

Once created, your **marketing tools** will be sent to your **media contacts** — book industry folks, long-lead reviewers, TV and radio stations, newspapers, libraries, magazines, online outlets, podcasters, reviewers and others — for two purposes: either to buy your book outright or to do a story about your book.

Said another way, **marketing tools** are what you use to carry out your **Marketing Plan.** We cover your **Marketing Plan** in the next section.

Marketing Tools: Meet the Media Kit

MARKETING OR PUBLICITY EXERCISE – TEST YOUR KNOWLEDGE

In general, marketing is an action you take to sell your book that may or may not result in someone buying your book or in writing a story about you or your book! Publicity is the result of a marketing activity — the actual story in a magazine or newspaper about your book or the actual podcast interview of you or your book.

Here is an example: We pitch to the local newspaper that we want to share THE secret that aspiring authors must know before they publish. If they know THE SECRET, their book will be SEEN and SOLD. The Newspaper Lifestyle columnist gets right back to us and, after a phone interview, publishes an article about the secret to successful publishing. In our example, the Pitch is the marketing, the resulting newspaper column is the publicity. Get it?

The following fun quiz tests your knowledge about the difference between marketing and publicity with tasks that may help promote and sell your book. It's an appetizer for the Marketing Tools and Marketing Plan discussion that follows. Good Luck!

IS IT MARKETING OR PUBLICITY?

Tasks:	Circle ONE
Send galley copies to industry reviewers	Marketing or Publicity
Send galley copies to magazine book reviewers	Marketing or Publicity
Send galley copies to newspaper reviewers	Marketing or Publicity
Submit book to publishing catalogs	Marketing or Publicity
Send book postcard to libraries	Marketing or Publicity
Pitch radio, tv, newspapers to do a story	Marketing or Publicity
Pitch bloggers to review / do a story	Marketing or Publicity
Pitch podcasters to review / do a story	Marketing or Publicity
Radio, TV, Newspaper story interview is published	Marketing or Publicity
Blogger review / story on you or your book posted	Marketing or Publicity
Industry review on your book published	Marketing or Publicity
Goodreads author Q&A session published	Marketing or Publicity
Instagram live episode	Marketing or Publicity
Facebook live session	Marketing or Publicity
Advertisement for your book or a speaking gig	Marketing or Publicity
Book signing	Marketing or Publicity
Press Release creation	Marketing or Publicity
Press Release distribution	Marketing or Publicity
Author Bio release creation	Marketing or Publicity
Author Q&A creation	Marketing or Publicity

Marketing Tools: Meet the Media Kit

Check your answers with the answer key at the end of the book. Great job! You are starting to learn the difference between marketing and publicity. **Marketing** is the plan and the completed tasks in the plan to sell the book. **Publicity** is the fruition of the plan when a story or interview is released about you or your book!

Both are important and there are endless marketing ideas out there. It is hard not to be overwhelmed. Take a breath. Now that you understand a little bit about the difference between marketing and publicity we are ready to move on to **Marketing Tools**.

Let's dive into creating the **Marketing Tools** that will enable you to market and publicize your book. Remember, once created, the marketing tools will be sent to your media contacts: long-lead reviewers, book industry folks, TV, newspapers, radio stations, libraries, magazines, online outlets, podcasters, reviewers, etc. to buy your book outright, to do a story about your book, to interview you, to do a story about something your book shares, and more.

WHAT IS A MEDIA KIT?

Part of the fun of publishing a book is the terminology that comes with publishing. When you know the terminology, you are part of the club! One of the most frequently used phrases in publishing, when it comes to book marketing, is the phrase **Media Kit**.

A Media Kit is a collection of several marketing pieces. These marketing pieces are created and written by you as a self-publisher to send out to industry and media contacts so that they can place an order for your book, get the word out about your book, review your book, or do a story about your book.

When publishing her first book, Claudine did not understand that the items selected for a Media Kit to be sent to a particular media contact does not have a set rule. The items selected to be sent are at the

> When we use the phrase "media contacts" we are referring to any entity or person including TV, radio, newspaper, magazine, as well as book industry reviewers and long-lead reviewers that a publisher decides to pitch with a Media Kit.

discretion of each publisher. or publicist. However, there are industry standards for each Media Kit item that must be present in order for your book to be taken seriously by the book industry and media.

Following are examples of Media Kit items that you can and should create to market your book. Once you understand the items in the Media Kit, it will become clear why certain items are sent to certain media. A typical Media Kit would include the following:

- **Press Release**
- **Author Bio**
- **Sell Sheet**
- **Brochure**
- **Interview Q&A**
- **Postcard**
- **Pitch / Cover letter**

Once your marketing tools are created and established, you can use them again and again to carry out the tasks on your Marketing Plan.

HOW TO USE YOUR MEDIA KIT

Let us say that one of the items on your **Marketing Plan** is to send a galley or Advance Reader Copy (ARC) of your book to an Industry Book Reviewer like *Foreword Magazine*. You would do the research on what *Foreword Magazine* requires you to submit for a book review. Specifically, you would print a copy of your **press release** on good bright

Marketing Tools: Meet the Media Kit

white paper stock and print a copy of your **Author Bio**. You would put the press release on top of the Author Bio and fold both papers in half at the middle. You would then put the folded papers on top of the galley and put the items you have carefully arranged in a clean, padded envelope, properly addressed, with a neat return address. In this example, you have selected a few pieces of your Media Kit to send to a book industry reviewer (a media contact).

NOTE: Some industry reviewers allow electronic galleys (review copies in a PDF format) to be submitted. This is wonderful news because it make it easier and less expensive to submit. This is also why it is so important to check the specific instructions for submission! You may also be allowed to send Media Kit items electronically.

Another example: Let's say that you have a radio show producer (a media contact) on your Marketing Plan to pitch to because you want them to interview you, feature your book, or do a story about the message in your book. You would select some items from your Media Kit to send to the radio producer. You could print the press release, author bio, interview questions and answers, as well as a cover letter pitch specifically addressed to the radio producer, and the galley or review copy of your book. You would stack the press release, author bio, interview questions in a pile and fold them all together at the middle. You would fold the cover letter pitch on top. You would place the folded papers on top of the galley or review copy and put the postcard INSIDE the galley. Then place the papers with the galley in a clean, padded envelope, addressed to the specific producer at the radio station, with a neat return address label.

Are you starting to understand the connection between Media Kit items and pitching to media contacts on your Marketing Plan and how they are all connected and somewhat flexible? Now let's get cracking on creating the marketing tools in your Media Kit.

Get Your Book Seen and Sold

THE POWERFUL PRESS RELEASE
The Heart of the Media Kit

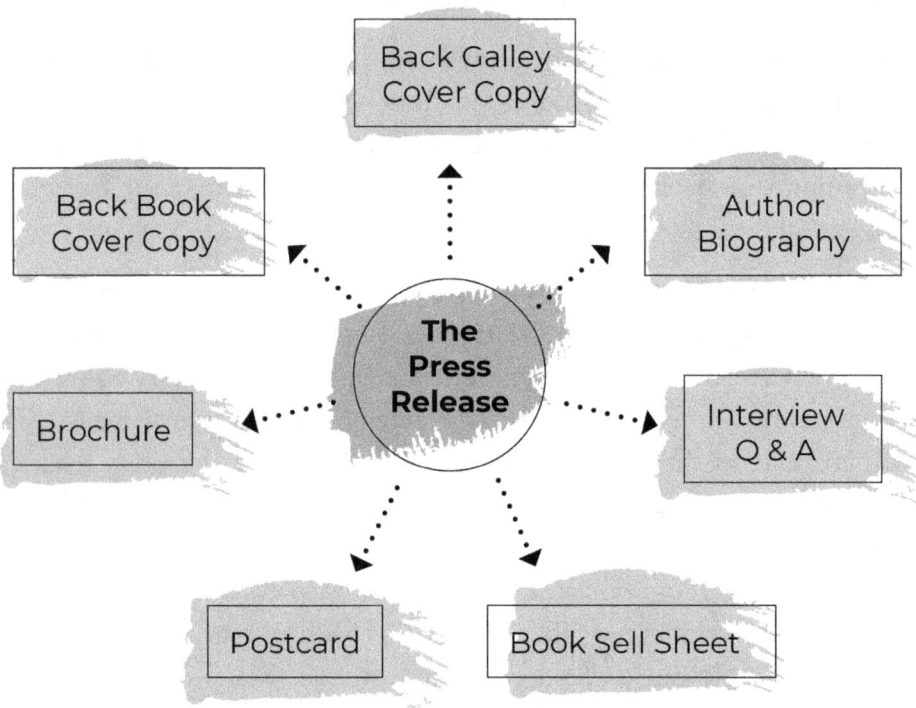

The Press Release with all the standard elements is the "well" from which all of your other media kit items (pieces) will be "watered." It is a critical tool in and of itself but it is also a resource to "draw from" and to use in all of your other media kits items as shown above.

THE POWERFUL PRESS RELEASE

The first and most important item in your Media Kit is the Press Release. Let us take a moment to appreciate the power of the Press Release. The Press Release is very special. You will use it again and again in your marketing efforts. The **Message, Audience, and Hook** work you did will help to create your Press Release. Once completed, the Press Release can be used to create the other items in your Media Kit such as your Author Biography, Interview Q&A, Sell Sheet, Postcard, Brochure, and the text for the back of your book cover, to name a few.

The Press Release is the perfect place to start when creating your marketing materials. As you can see from the powerful Press Release graphic, the information from the Press Release feeds all the other marketing tools. The time spent to create a stellar Press Release will be well worth your effort.

NOTE: If you have a traditional publisher, their publicity department will most likely be creating the Press Release. Your input based on the work you have done on **Message, Audience and Hook** will be valuable to your assigned publicist.

WHAT IS A PRESS RELEASE?

You have certainly seen press releases. Companies and governments use press releases to get information out to the media. The press release is the announcement of a story. You will use a press release in a similar way to announce the release of your book.

The press release is a marketing tool that must be written in an industry standard way. There are elements to a well-written and effective press release that we will review with you. These elements MUST be present to be accepted by the book industry. When all the correct elements are in the press release, the media contact knows exactly where to look on it to find the information they will include in the story. If the elements are not where they are supposed to be, the media contact will quickly lose interest.

LET'S GET STARTED

> The Press Release is written in the third person, as if from a publicist, not directly from you.

A press release is the world's first exposure to your book and to you. The best advice that we ever heard for the creation of a good press release is that in **one page** it tells a riveting story. It includes the who, what, where, when, and why – the 5 W's. We add a "How." The content of the press release identifies a problem and your book is the answer; or it highlights a riveting story that the reader simply cannot miss and the reason why the reader cannot miss it.

For fiction, the press release summarizes the plot of your book so well that the reader cannot wait to get their hands on it.

The goal of any press release is for the media contact who reads it to feel that they have enough information in the press release to do a story, and perhaps to want more. The press release will include the technical information for the book and contact information for your publicist. The reader will know exactly how to purchase your book or how to contact you for an interview.

A press release will usually be written and re-written many times before a final version is produced, so do not be nervous to get started. With each revision or rearrangement of copy from top to bottom or bottom to top, you will be making it better. It is part of the process. All of the work that you did in **Message, Audience, and Hook** will be useful in creating a great press release.

On page 106, you will see a copy of the Press Release for the first self-published version of Claudine's book.

Marketing Tools: Meet the Media Kit

THE ANATOMY OF THE PRESS RELEASE

<<Publisher Name>> Contact: <<name>>
For Immediate Release publicist@gmail.com

Fabulous, Interesting, Eye-Catching Headline

HEADLINE: Your press release headline must grab attention. You are telling a story and you need to get the media contact interested immediately. Make it pithy, creative and clever. Give the reader a reason to read the rest of the press release.

FIRST PARAGRAPH: Don't wait to get to the good stuff here. This paragraph may be the only paragraph a media contact reads and it has to be fantastic. **What** is the problem your book solves? **Why** is the problem important and worth solving? What is interesting about the way you solved the problem with your book? Keep it positive and interesting.

SECOND PARAGRAPH: Say how your book solves the problem you presented in the first paragraph and include a quote by the author that gets to the heart of reason why the author feels the need to share their message with their book. You could also include a blurb quote from a positive review you may have gotten from another author or expert.

THIRD PARAGRAPH: Introduce your book's title (publisher, pub date/month, year, price, format) with more description of the book and what is in it. Add some details with the unique things that the book includes and how it is written.

FOURTH PARAGRAPH: A bit more detail of how you wrote the book. What methods you used to put it together. Share specific aspects of the book that could be stand-alone stories.

FIFTH PARAGRAPH: Introduce the author and her bona fides. Highlight her writing history and where she is published. Include any stand-out accomplishments on social media and where she can be found online. Add any professional affiliations that are related and how she is an expert in the field. Add any professional affiliations that are related and how she is an expert in the field. Add one personal blurb, where the author lives, for example.

Finally, include information about the book itself so that the reader does not have go back and search for it in the press release.

Title:	**ISBN:**
Author:	**Price:**
Pages:	**Pub Date:**

WORKBOOK EXERCISE: CREATE YOUR PRESS RELEASE

Answer the following questions to identify the key messages and hooks to include in your press release. Then start a Word document and create your own press release. Use **The Anatomy of The Press Release,** on the previous page, as your guide and start writing. As you write, continue to ask and answer the question, "Why will a media contact care?"

PRESS RELEASE QUESTIONS

Who are you trying to reach or help? Your specific target audience for this answer (**Audience**)

What is the issue that your book solves?
OR
What is unique or fantastic about your book? (**Message and Hook**)

Where can a journalist find you for an interview or story quote? (publicist or acting publicist contact)

When is your book being released and where can people order and/or find it?

Why is your book the solution to the problem? Why are you the person to write this book? Why should a reader pick up your novel? (**Message and/or Hook**)

How does your book solve the problem? How were you able to solve the problem? How did you come up with the idea for your fantastic novel? (**Message and/or Hook**)

OTHER MEDIA KIT ITEMS

There are other Media Kit items that you could create and use in your book marketing efforts. Here are the most popular Media Kit options with a brief description of each. Be sure to refer to the powerful press release to pull what is appropriate into each Media Kit item. Remember, the press release has your most powerful, persuasive and scintillating hooks and copy. Also include what you documented in your message exercises. The pieces in the Media Kit provide you with the opportunity to add more details about the book and additional story ideas.

Author Bio: Here is where you describe yourself and your accomplishments in detail. Keep it to one sheet and include a professional headshot. Talk about your book in the first paragraph — why you wrote it, who it helps, and how you did it. Include a personal quote. Are you also a speaker? Where have you spoken, especially as it relates to the material in your book? Are you a writer? Where were you published? Do you have a community service project that is dear to you? Does your Instagram account have many followers? Anything unique or different about you? Did you graduate from college at fifteen or invent a product that was sold on QVC? Give **media contacts** a reason to reach out to you for an interview or a story. Finally, in the last paragraph, add a few professional tidbits — where you studied, where you have worked, professional affiliations, board memberships, where you live, something about your family, etc. Be sure to include the way to contact you or a publicist representative.

Book Sell Sheet: This sell sheet is all about the book, a book overview. Re-read what you wrote for the press release. Include a hi-resolution picture of your book cover on the sell sheet. Tell the reader all they will need to know about the book. Share what is in the book, the problem it solves, and how it solves it. Bullet points that list what the reader will find in the book can be very effective. Use the hook in the press release to highlight the book. Again, we want the media contact who reads it to want to do a story about the book, to mention the book, to highlight the book, or to feature you as an expert on the book's subject matter. For a novel, include endorsement quotes. The final paragraph can include a mini-bio of you, the author, described in third person. Be sure to include the way to contact you or a representative publicist, as well as the technical information about the book (publisher, release date, ISBN, price, number of pages).

Brochure/Flyer: A brochure is a Media Kit item that "advertises" your book. It will include the information on the press release highlighting the book's hooks, audience, genre and its technical information (Publisher, release date, ISBN, price, number of pages) A brochure is a Media Kit item used to advertise the book directly to libraries and bookstores, for example.

Interview Q&A: This is a Media Kit item that could be sent to potential reviewers of your book and/or journalists who may want to interview you. YOU come up with the questions and also provide the answers. A provocative Q&A gives the potential interviewer or journalist ideas of stories to pursue with you. A well-written and interesting Q&A makes a journalist's job easy! Writing a Q&A is also a great exercise for an author. By taking the time to come up with potential interview ideas and answering them as well, you may uncover new story ideas never before considered. For the radio, TV, or Podcast journalist or interviewer, you expand additional story possibilities based on what is included in the press release and sell sheet.

Postcard: A postcard is a Media Kit item that is also an advertisement. A postcard with a hi-res picture of the cover of the book, a couple of pithy descriptions of the book, a few blurbs or endorsements, as well as the book's technical information can be sent to mailing lists. Mailing lists of media contact targets can be purchased along with mailing labels. For example, a mailing list of parenting magazines would be the perfect target for a book to help new moms. A mailing list of libraries or independent bookstores might also be perfect for your postcard. The postcard can also be handed out at speaking engagements, book signings, or simply placed in the review copy of the book.

Now that you have your Media Kit items ready to go, it's time for the **Marketing Plan!**

MARKETING PLAN – PLUS THE SECRET

Let's dive into creating the Marketing Plan that will guide you to market and publicize your book.

Again, if you decide to publish your book traditionally, your publisher will create a Marketing Plan (with your input) and will carry out some of the tasks in the plan. It is important for you to understand the plan and to be an advocate for your book. Make sure that outreach to book industry and long-lead reviewers are part of your Marketing Plan. Your tasks in the Marketing Plan will keep you very busy as well. If you are self-publishing, your job will be to create the Marketing Plan and carry out **all** the tasks on it.

TAKING THE SCARY OUT OF A MARKETING PLAN

We know that the term "Marketing Plan" may seem a bit intimidating and time consuming. It sounds so very formal, doesn't it? First of all, call your plan whatever you want. If "Marketing Plan" makes you antsy, call it a **list** or an **outline** or even a **TaDah! List**. It doesn't matter what you call it. What matters is what it is.

A book Marketing Plan is simply a list of actions / tasks that you decide you are going to do to get your book SEEN and SOLD.

Mom used to always say, "Work your list!" Work your list to get your book seen and sold.

THE MOST IMPORTANT PART OF YOUR MARKETING PLAN: THE SECRET

In the introduction of this book, we promised to reveal **The Secret**. You need to know the most important task for successful bookselling ahead of your book publication. Stay with us.

Note: Don't panic if you are reading this book and you have already published your book! As we have discussed previously, there are many more ways to market your book and you can save what you're about to learn now for your next book!

Because you are selling a book and you want the world to see and buy it, you need a part of your Marketing Plan to be **specifically for the book industry**. Who makes up the book industry? The book industry includes book industry reviewers, long-lead reviewers, libraries, bookstores, book catalogs, etc. These book industry entities need to know about your book well **BEFORE** your publication date so they can review your book, add it to their catalogs, write stories about your book, or order your book for their inventory *well before its release date!*

The *New York Times Book Review* is an example of a book industry long-lead reviewer. They only review books **that will be newly released.** They need your review copy well in advance of your publication date so that the staff has the time to read the book, decide whether to review it, write the review, and then publish the review in the month your book is published (or released). Think of the exposure for your book if the *New York Times* decided to review it! The only thing you had to do was take the time to send them a review copy of your book as they requested, four months in advance of publication!

Book catalogs are another example. It takes time to create and print a catalog of thousands of books for potential buyers, specifically bookstores and libraries, that then gets mailed to potential buyers.

These catalogs need your review copy and book information in order to include your book in their catalogs well in advance of publication.

Here is another example. *People Magazine* has a "book pick" section. They only include new releases. Again, their editors need time to select your book, review it, write it up, and get it in their magazine BEFORE your book is published!

Once again, the book industry needs to get your review copy and Media Kit materials four to five months in advance of your publication date. If you miss this deadline, the book industry will NOT know about your book and will therefore not review your book. Most book industry reviewers do NOT review books AFTER they publish. NEVER. EVER. EVER.

Without industry reviews, your book will not get the exposure it deserves. You only get one shot at this, but it is so, so easy to get it right! Follow the directions of the reviewers and meet their deadlines.

Because this step of your Marketing Plan is so important, we will include a list of suggested book industry and long-lead reviewers to get you started. The list is by no means complete and you must research each one for updated submission information and instructions because they change all the time. There are also other parts to your Marketing Plan. As an example, we included the Book Marketing Plan for Claudine's first book in the Exhibits.

BEGIN YOUR MARKETING PLAN

To begin a Marketing Plan for **YOUR** book, start a Word document and title it *Marketing Plan*. Whew! You are halfway there.

It is important to remember that no two Marketing Plans are the same. If you decided to traditionally publish, you might see a very long and detailed Marketing Plan. If you are self-publishing, as Claudine did with her first book, she included the marketing tasks that she could reasonably (and affordably) do.

After the **Marketing Plan** section where you decide **what media** you would like to target, we provide an exercise for you to decide who you will target ... your **media contact list**.

MARKETING PLAN

Below is a very simple **Marketing Plan**. Remember that no Marketing Plan is set in stone. It is flexible. Take some time to think about the tasks that you feel will be the most impactful to sell your book. We, of course, feel that the outreach to the book industry reviewers is a must!

> Review copy, galley, and ARC (Advance Readers Copy) are publishing terms that mean the same thing — a review copy.

Pre-Publication — 4-5 months in advance of your publication date.
- Send Galleys (review copies) to **Book Industry reviewers**. Book industry reviewers include *Kirkus, Foreword, Booklist*, etc. See list included at the end of the chapter.

- Send Galleys (review copies) to **Long-Lead Reviewers**. "Long-lead" because they take a long time to read and review your book BEFORE it's published. Long-lead reviewers include *People Magazine, Slate Magazine, The New York Times*.

- **Book Awards.** Submit your book for a book award. Google "book awards" for possible places to enter your book.

- **Endorsement Outreach.** Send review copies to other authors, friends, experts in your field for an endorsement blurb.

- **Bookstores and Libraries.** Send brochure/postcard with Media Kit to book catalogs used by libraries and bookstores for new title purchases.

2-3 months in advance of your publication date.

- Send Media Kits to targeted national and regional long-lead magazines for an interview or mentions.
- Send Media Kits to targeted national and regional long-lead newspapers for an interview or mention.

1 month in advance of your publication date

- Send Media Kits to targeted national and regional long-lead radio stations for an interview or mention.
- Send Media Kits to targeted national and regional long-lead TV stations for an interview or mention.
- Pitch book review or subject matter specific **podcasts** for review or mention.
- Pitch book review or subject-matter-specific **blogs** for review or mention.

NOTE: You may be wondering why you pitch to radio and TV stations, podcasts, and book review blogs just one month before publication. The reason is because if one of those outlets agrees to do a story on you and/or your book, it will be aired soon after. You want to make sure your book is available for sale BEFORE your interview airs. How frustrating would it be to a potential book buyer who hears about your book from a radio show and has to wait to buy it? You may have just lost a sale!

Author Outreach at Publication Date

These are additional Marketing Plan items, the tasks that you personally can do to promote your book.

- Newsletter announcement
- Your website announcement
- Facebook Live Book Launch
- Instagram Live Book Launch

- Goodreads Book Launch
- Tik Tok Announcement
- LinkedIn, Pinterest, Twitter, Threads, Facebook announcements

Again, for all of these actions, make sure the book is available for sale!

Other possibilities for Publicity when book is published

- Press release syndication
- Paid advertisement
- Book club appearance
- Book signings
- Speaking gigs
- Book trade shows: research and book in advance — weigh the cost

Consider Special Sales

Would your book be a great addition to a specialty store? Perhaps you wrote a book about tarot card reading and there is a holistic store in town. Pitch your book to the store. Offer to give a reading there.

MEDIA CONTACT LIST EXERCISE - FIND THE RIGHT FIT FOR YOUR PITCH

If you have read any "how to market your book" posts, articles, books, or attended workshops, you have come across the phrase **media contacts**. We have already used the phrase a few times in this workbook. When Claudine first read the phrase in *Dan Poynter's Self-Publishing Manual* and later in book marketing courses, she didn't understand what it meant. She thought that "media contacts" was a list that was published somewhere that was accessible to everyone. She thought that she could purchase it or find it and use it. What she failed to grasp was that **media contacts** is a list of people that YOU create, that is unique to you.

The concept of creating your very own media contact list may seem a little daunting, but it is exciting, too. It's exciting because it's an opportunity to use your unique grasp of the message that you want to share with a media outlet. By media outlet we mean an editor, producer, or journalist for a newspaper, magazine, blog or website, or a personality who is on TV, the radio, or a podcast.

Next is an exercise to help you to identify **your** media contacts. The beauty of it is that YOU get to decide your own media contact list. It is a list of people across different areas of the media who you will contact and ask if they would like to do a story, a review or a mention of your book or of you. Your Marketing Plan is your guide. If you have "pitch to magazines" on your Marketing Plan, you need to identify some magazine media contacts. Your media contact list is dynamic. There will be additions and changes. Most pitches will be made through email.

There are resources for sale online that provide media contact data locally and by region for radio, TV, newspapers, and magazines. Specifically, the data includes hundreds of contacts with names, emails and mailing addresses. Before you contact one of these people, make sure they are still at the job.

Beware: Some are quite costly and provide little return.

MEDIA CONTACT WORKSHEET

Find the Right Fit For Your Pitch

Newspapers – Local

_____

_____

Newspapers – National

_____

Search for editors and journalists in the following sections: book review, lifestyle, health, business, entertainment, food. Plus: Does YOUR book have a local story angle?

Radio – Local

_____

_____

Radio – National

_____

Search for editors, producers and journalists who work on: talk shows, interview shows, how-to shows, business shows, health advice shows, job & career advice shows, political shows, religious, and psychology shows.

TV – Local

_____

_____

TV – National

_____

Search editors, producers and journalists who work on: morning talk shows, lifestyle segments, politics, economics, book reviews, and one-on-one interviews.

Get Your Book Seen and Sold

Magazines – Local

_____

_____

Magazines – National

_____

_____

Identify media contacts by magazine genre AND search for editors, journalists in magazines with a book review section, lifestyle, beauty, health, relationships, current events, food, gardening, fashion, teaching, or psychology. You will never look at a magazine rack in the grocery store the same way again!

Podcasts

_____

_____

Search on the podcast platforms (Apple, Spotify) by topic to find podcasts to pitch: book review, interview, women's issues, social, health, business, entrepreneur, true crime, lifestyle, health, history, relationship advice, nutrition, parenting, women's issues, etc.

Blogs

_____

_____

Search online for blogs by topic: book review, women book review, book summary, women issues, health, yoga, relationships, hobbies, outdoor, parenting, food, family, fiction books, beauty, fashion, female entrepreneur, book marketing, etc.

Websites

_____

_____

_____

_____

Search on line for websites that accept submissions for book reviews and/or book clubs. Search for topic-specific websites: parenting, relationships, entrepreneurs, new moms, book lovers, fashion, religion, lifestyle, computers, cooking, or any other categories that work for you.

One item on your Marketing Plan is to pitch to local radio. You now need to identify a local radio station to find a show and the producer of that radio show who would be a good fit to do an interview, review, or story about your book and/or you. The name of the radio show and producer is your first media contact!

PITCHING TO YOUR MEDIA CONTACTS

Let's recap. You have your **Marketing Plan** and your **media contacts** identified. Now you are ready to pitch to your selected **media contacts**.

Remember, you know your message better than anyone, and you are more passionate about your message than anyone and you want to get your message out more than anyone. This means that you will come up with the most creative and unique media to contact to pitch your message. You are going to include the usual suspects on your media contacts list, too. However, you will use your passion and your knowledge to look beyond the usual.

Below is an example of how your hunch about a **media contact** can pay great rewards.

When coming up with media contacts for her first book, Claudine thought that the nationally syndicated radio show for Dr. Laura Schlessinger would be a perfect fit. She had a hunch that the message in her book hit the right chord of honesty and humor that Dr. Laura loves. She identified a media contact — the producer of the Dr Laura Schlessinger show. She did not send an email pitch to the producer, however. She sent a review copy of her book along with a press release, author bio, interview Q&A, and a one-page sell sheet to the producer, along with a cover letter where she said exactly why she thought Dr. Laura might like the book. She also included some bullet points to highlight the humor and honest advice found in the book.

Claudine was right. Dr. Laura liked the book and she highlighted it on a segment of her radio program where she gave away books to listeners who requested it. Because the show was nationally syndicated, Claudine's book ranked #1 on Amazon's parenting genre for that day. She also asked Dr. Laura if she could quote what was said about the book on the radio show as a blurb for future promotion. Dr. Laura agreed and her quote "this book is helpful and a hoot" is on the second edition of the book. Do not underestimate a personal gut feeling. It can lead to fantastic results. Take the time to do the work in this workbook to unleash the best ideas of where to market your book. It cost Claudine nothing to come up with that media contact.

PITCHING TIPS

When you pitch to a media contact, remember to use the same method you used to pitch agents or publishers. Go on their website and look for the instructions for pitching. Can you email the media contact directly? Do they want an email pitch or a press release? Do they want it as an attachment to an email or do they want it embedded in the email? Specific instructions, if there are any, are very important. It can be a huge turnoff for a producer, editor, or journalist if they specifically state how they want to see pitches and you do not follow their instructions.

EMAIL PITCH TIPS

The subject line on your email pitch may be the only words that your media contact reads. Make it good, pithy and short enough that the media contact can read it without opening the email.

If you are pitching to a book reviewer, it is okay to add a call to action in the message line — something like "**Book Review Opportunity: Secret to Newborn Baby Sleep.**"

In the body of the email, invite the media contact to review your new book. Use your other Media Kit items to bullet point the most exciting aspects of your book. If you have any blurb quotes from experts or other authors, include one or two. Corroborating evidence of the greatness of your book can be persuasive. Use bullet points to highlight the most salient parts of your book. Let the media contact know how to get in touch with you or your publicist and that you will promptly send a review copy or email an e-galley.

Finally, follow-up. If you hear nothing back in a week, send another email. This time in the subject line add the words "Gentle Reminder" or "In case you missed it" and repeat the original subject line. **"Gentle reminder. Book Review Opportunity: Secret to Newborn Baby Sleep."**

Cut and paste the same original email pitch, but add *"In case you missed it . . ."* at the top of the email before the greeting.

We cannot tell you how many times this second pitch yields results. Emails get lost and forgotten all the time. Frequently, a nice gentle reminder does the trick.

If the media contact does not respond after the second pitch, we suggest stopping there. You do not want to be a pest. If you come up with a new story angle or a new book down the road, try again months later.

To pitch to a producer or journalist, the subject line is slightly different. The call to action is not a review but a story opportunity. The subject line must entice. Something like: **"Story Opportunity: Mom Solves Newborn Baby Sleep Issues."**

The editor of a parenting magazine would be too tempted NOT to read this pitch! It would be journalistic malpractice if the problem of newborn baby sleep were solved and not publicized. Am I right? You get the idea. The subject line does not read "New Baby Book Release." It entices with a solution to a worldwide problem. In the body of the pitch use bullet points to highlight the great stuff in the book.

Finally, your call to action in the email is, "The author is available for interview. Thank you for your consideration for interview or mention."

Hopefully, the editor will contact your publicist. Sometimes the editor may simply ask for a cover image of your book and your press release and simply "mention" you in their magazine. That works, right?

Don't forget to follow up with a gentle reminder if you do not receive an email back.

Finally, on the next page we have added what we promised as **The Secret**. These are the long-lead book industry reviewers and a checklist for you to follow to track your completion and progress with each. Remember that the contact information and instructions for submission change all the time so you must check each "submission" requirement on their website before you submit.

Marketing Plan: Plus THE SECRET

"THE SECRET"

Industry Book Reviewer Checklist

Kirkus Reviews

Kirkusreviews.com
"Submission Guidelines"

When? 4-5 months before Pub Date
What? Printed or Digital Galley

Sent Galley _____ Date _____
Receipt Notice _____ Date _____
Review? ☐ Yes ☐ No

Notes:
▸ Submit to specific contact
▸ Submit by publisher only

Foreword Magazine

publishers.forewordreviews.com
"Get Your Book Reviewed"

When? 4 months before Pub Date
What? Digital Galleys or PDF **ONLY**

Sent Galley _____ Date _____
Receipt Notice _____ Date _____
Review? ☐ Yes ☐ No

Notes:
▸ Specific submission info required
▸ Clarion Review for purchase option

Publisher's Weekly (PW)

PublishersWeekly.com
"Submission Guidelines"

When? 3-4 months before 1st day of publication month
What? Digital galley via GalleyTracker
Or print galley (2 copies required)

Sent Galley _____ Date _____
Receipt Notice _____ Date _____
Review? ☐ Yes ☐ No

Notes:
▸ Finished books ARE allowed
▸ US distribution required

Booklist – ALA & Booklist Online

booklistonline.com
"Get Reviewed"

When? 15 weeks prior to publication
What? Digital galley preferred

Sent Galley _____ Date _____
Receipt Notice _____ Date _____
Review? ☐ Yes ☐ No

Notes:
▸ eBook ONLY submissions allowed
▸ Finished copies requested

"THE SECRET"

Industry Book Reviewer Checklist

Library Journal
Libraryjournal.com
"Review Submissions"

When? 6 Months Prior to Pub Date
What? Digital or Print Galley

Sent Galley _____ Date _____
Receipt Notice _____ Date _____
Review? ☐ Yes ☐ No

Notes:
▸ Finished Books may be sent if properly noted

American Book Review
AmericanBookReview.org
"Frequently Asked Questions"

When? 3- 4 Months Prior to Pub
What? Digital or Print Galley

Sent Galley _____ Date _____
Receipt Notice _____ Date _____
Review? ☐ Yes ☐ No

Notes:
▸ ABR specializes in "frequently neglected works" – described on site

---

NY Times Book Review
Help.nytimes.com
"Book Review"

When? 3 Months Prior to Pub Date
What? PDF of the Galley

Sent Galley _____ Date _____
Receipt Notice _____ Date _____
Review? ☐ Yes ☐ No

Notes:
▸ Email galley to:
  bookassisstant@nytimes.com

BookPage
BookPage.com
"Submission Guidelines"

When? 3 Months Prior to Pub Date
What? Print galley or digital galley

Sent Galley _____ Date _____
Receipt Notice _____ Date _____
Review? ☐ Yes ☐ No

Notes:
▸ Digital and print galleys sent to specific contacts on the site

DISTINCTIVE BOOK MARKETING IDEAS
INTRODUCTION

You must know by now that there are unlimited book marketing ideas out there. The number of things that you could do to market your book can be overwhelming. Instead of looking at that fact as a downer, try looking at it positively. There will always be another marketing idea you can try to get your book seen and sold!

Common sense tells us that you simply cannot try all of the possible marketing ideas out there. In this chapter, we review a few tips and a few places where we think you will get the best marketing bang for your time. Remember, you have already analyzed your book's **message, audience and hook**. Go back and review your results. It is in your hard work that you will find your audience and make the best decisions about where, when and how to pitch your book. We honestly believe that YOU will come up with the best ideas to pitch and market your book.

EMBRACE THE CONCEPT OF TARGETED MARKETING

When an author markets their book, the first place that usually comes to mind is social media. You may have noticed that we did not dedicate a chapter to social media. One reason is because a whole book would be needed to cover marketing on social media, but there is another more important reason. While social media is a great place to get exposure for your book, it is also a TIMESUCK — a never-ending pull of learning, researching, posting, following, responding, picture-taking, video-taking, editing, and learning on platforms that are saturated. We feel that social media is a great tool, but especially when used in the *most effective way.*

THE TRICK TO SUCCESSFUL SOCIAL MEDIA MARKETING IS TARGET AND TALENT

You have already taken the time to find your audience, correct? Identify the social media channels (one or two) where you are most likely to find your specific target audience. Consider your personal talents: Do you take pictures? Are you good with graphics? Do you know how to record and edit audio? Are you good with videos? Do you write? (Of course you do . . . you just wrote a book!) Are you a speaker? Are you funny? What are your talents and what do you like to do?

The most effective way to use social media to market your book is to **target** your marketing efforts on a couple of social media channels that enhance your **talents.**

One: When you target your focus on a few social media channels, you will centralize activity, thereby garnering a bigger audience and buzz. With more eyes on your book there will be more potential sales.

Two: Your marketing efforts will not seem like work because you are good at it and you enjoy it and will be motivated to keep doing it.

SOCIAL MEDIA MARKETING TARGETED STRATEGY

When you start to market and promote your book, a **targeted strategy** is SOOO much better than spreading your content across **all** social media platforms. Once you establish a presence and audience in one social media channel you can try another and branch out. The added bonus to a targeted social media strategy is that your results will be **measurable**. For example, with two active social media channels, you can determine what is working and decide to stick with it or try a different channel. Leveraging your talents, and hopefully your interest, will add to the **authenticity of your content** that is the special sauce to reach your audience!

Enter your Specific Target Audience here.

What are the social media channels where your Specific Target Market spends a lot of time?

What are the social media channels you like, find pleasurable, or that showcase your skills?

Hopefully there is an intersection where your audience spends time and where you like to spend time. Focus your efforts on the intersection!

ONLINE MARKETING IMPERATIVES

We believe that although the best strategy for marketing online is a targeted strategy, there are a few **Online Marketing Imperatives** you must do to successfully market your book!

Website: An author must have a website to direct media and readers. Your website does not have to be expensive, but clean and professional is the way to go. **Squarespace** and **WordPress**, for example, are clean, inexpensive website/blog platforms. You will need the basics on your website. First, you will need a tab for media that includes a publicity contact, a downloadable press release, and a downloadable book cover. A tab that includes specific book information is also a must. The book tab page would include a high-resolution picture of your book cover and a link to purchase your book online. It might also include the details of your book, as well as reviews, endorsements, and blurbs. A blog is nice, too. There, you, as the author, can write about your book journey, where you will be able to promote your book, and continue to add expert advice.

> To learn the best way to utilize the social media channel you picked to market your book, research it. In your browser's search bar type "best tips to use Goodreads to market your book" or "is LibraryThing worth it to market your book" or "how to use Instagram to market your book." You will be shocked by the number of articles written on the subject that are specific to book marketing.

Pick a social media channel: Select one or two channels (Facebook, Instagram, Twitter, Pinterest, Threads, TikTok, LinkedIn). Decide on the channel where your target audience hangs out. Learn how to properly and most efficiently use the channel you picked. Does it work best with audio and video posts? Do you need hashtags? If so, research the proper use of them. Do you need to "tag" other users? Focus on the channel you picked when you add new content and updates. Do not forget to interact with other users.

Amazon: Amazon, as a social media channel, and it *is* a social media channel, gets a big section all of its own. We feel it is your third imperative online marketing channel.

NOTE: The tips mentioned below can be applied to other book retailer sites (i.e., B&N, Apple Books, Bookbub) and social media channels (Goodreads, Facebook, Instagram, Pinterest, etc.)

AMAZON IS A POWERFUL SOCIAL MEDIA CHANNEL

When we think of social media we think of Facebook, Instagram, Twitter, Goodreads, and more recently, Threads. Amazon does not come to mind at first, but Amazon is a powerful social media tool. Early in book marketing for her first book, Claudine had some great advice from the interior designer she hired. His book services company did it all: interior design, cover design, and editing. He was also a wealth of book marketing information and allowed her to bend his ear with many questions. Once piece of advice that really resonated was to use Amazon as the *tool* that it is to get exposure for her book.

How is Amazon a tool? First, Amazon is always highly ranked in search engines. Think of how many times you Google a book title. Every time you search for a book title an Amazon link comes up close to the top or at the very top of the search results, right? Right! Second, Amazon offers ways for authors to interact with book buyers and potential book buyers through the Author Page. Remember, book readers are book buyers! Now that you know that Amazon is a powerful social media tool, how can you use it to market and promote your book?

AUTHOR INFORMATION PAGE ON AMAZON

Most likely you will be selling your book on Amazon. Every author that adds a book on Amazon will be able to set up an "author page" where you can add your picture, your book information, a bio of yourself including a website where you can be found. Get the idea? If someone searches for you or your book on Amazon and they find your book, they will also see your name. Your name is a hyperlink to your author page on Amazon. When they click your name to get to your author page, you want the page to have something on it, don't you? How sad is it when you find a book on Amazon, click the author's name and the only thing on it is the phantom picture instead of a beautiful face. So sad. Step one, once your book is up on Amazon, is to fill out the author information on your author page. Take the time to upload a headshot, add a bio, and include your email and/or website. The Amazon author page is free publicity and it is easy to fill out.

AMAZON BOOK PAGE INFO

If you are self-publishing, make sure your book's page has information that you, as publisher, can add, including a description of the book, and reviews/blurbs/awards that your book has earned. There is also a way to create an author interview and a way to upload a video about your book on your book page.

Note: If you have a traditional publisher, they will fill out the information for you. However, it is always good to read what the publisher has added for completeness and to share news of updates, reviews, awards, etc. with your publisher so that they can promptly update your book's page.

AMAZON REVIEWS

Another way to get some exposure for your book is to review other books! What do we mean? When you sign into your personal Amazon account you can review other people's books and your name will be associated with the review. In years past, you were able to include your book's title as part of your name. In that way, your name and book title would be attributed to the review in a hyperlink. Amazon took away the ability to add your book title and/or website to your name, but you can still add your name that is hyperlinked to your Amazon Author Page. Here's an example of how this could be powerful.

Claudine wrote a book for new moms to help them with their first baby — baby care and transition to motherhood tips — with honesty and humor. If you are a parent, think of how many books you read about pregnancy, parenting, and motherhood. If you are like either of us, you have shelves full of them. We can agree that parents buy many books. Claudine read many parenting and pregnancy books similar to hers and then reviewed them on Amazon. Her potential audience of book buyers who pursue similar books might see her review and click on her name and see and purchase HER book! See how that works? It may sound time-consuming, but chances are you have already read many books in your subject area and can add your thoughts without too much trouble. Anytime an Amazon reader clicks on one of your reviews, they will see you, your bio, your book, your website and the other reviews you have done. They will also see your Amazon Lists and Amazon Gift Guides.

AMAZON LISTS AND GIFT GUIDES

As we mentioned, Amazon is a social media site and the way to be social and included in the Amazon rankings is to add content. Adding reviews of books, or even products, is one way to add content. Another way is to add an Amazon List or an Amazon Gift Guide. These ideas for content are a bit time-consuming, but once done they are evergreen and connected directly to you on Amazon. Plus, you may quickly be able to put the lists and guides together because you are already interested in the subject matter. The benefit is that anyone who finds you will also find these lists. Plus, Amazon may promote your list or guide on their own. Free exposure is a possibility.

For example, Claudine created a list of great books for new moms — of course she included her own book that, by the way, had been dubbed "the best baby shower gift" by Amazon reviewers! But you don't have to include your own book. The idea is to provide valuable content in your subject area, so your audience can find you and your book.

AMAZON REVIEWS OF YOUR BOOK

While you can write reviews of other books in your subject matter, asking for fair, unpaid reviews from your fans and book readers is an important way to increase the ranking of your book on Amazon. An increased ranking means more eyes on your book... and more sales.

A WARNING: NEGATIVE BOOK REVIEWS

There are negative book reviews. It comes with the territory. Sometimes the reviews can be hurtful, unfair, and just plain untrue. After years of watching Amazon reviews, we have seen the good, the bad, and the ugly.

A few rules to consider: An author NEVER responds to a bad review with a rebuttal comment. It is bad form. Period. As hard as it is to not defend your book, you must resist. It looks bad to defend it in a comment.

Amazon never (or almost never) retracts a negative review so do not waste your energy. You have other positive marketing ideas that need your attention. Move on. Understand that sometimes "haters gotta hate" and that is how it is. It can be clear from some reviews that the reviewer never read the book. There is nothing to be done. If there is anything to be gleaned from a negative review, glean it and apply it to your next book.

Also, remember that any publicity is good publicity, even a bad review. In fact, it is the number of reviews that boost your ranking. That applies to eBooks (Kindle) as well. So, encourage your readers to leave a review whether they like your book or not!

Here is a funny story so you don't feel bad if it happens to you. After Claudine's first book was published, a woman sent her a letter with a brochure on how to get help for her depression! Depression? She was simply writing about honesty in motherhood! Some people have no sense of humor. In one Amazon review, a reviewer said that she should not have kids if she was going to complain about it! Ha! Humor and honesty are great ways to cope with motherhood! What is the matter with being honest about how much hard work motherhood is?

Please take our advice and don't take bad reviews to heart. In contrast, the number of reviews that the book received where moms thanked her for tips and for sharing that they are not alone, far outweighed the negative reviews.

We have included a few ways to take advantage of the social media channel that is Amazon! New opportunities for authors are being added every day so be sure to continue to research it.

MORE REMARKABLE MARKETING IDEAS
TRICKS TO IDENTIFY MEDIA CONTACTS FOR BOOK REVIEWS, AUTHOR INTERVIEW, OR MENTION

We discussed creating a media contacts list and sending pitches for review, interview or mention, remember?

Create a Media Contact "list to pitch" from the Internet

Search the internet for similar book titles and authors' names. For example, if you wrote a cookbook about French cooking, search French Cookbooks. Do a new search of each cookbook you found by typing: "The Title of the French Cookbook" and "Book Review".

The results will be online websites, blogs, podcasts, and magazines that did a book review on that book! Select a few, identify their media contact information and book review submission instructions and pitch to them!

Easy peasy, right? If the website posted a review of a French cookbook, perhaps they will post a review of YOUR French cookbook!

You can search the Author of the French Cookbook in the same way.

Search: "Author Name" with "Interview" or "Author Name" with "Book Review" or "Author Name" with "Podcast Interview".

The results will be online websites, blogs, podcasts and magazines that interviewed the author. Perhaps they would like to interview you, too! Select a few, identify their media contact information and pitch away!

Create a Media Contact "list to pitch" From Your Bookshelf

Take a look at your personal bookshelf. One of our favorite tricks (and it is just fun to do) is to look inside any good book, a book that you like, and a book that may be like yours. Most trade books begin with pages of blurbs or testimonials — little reviews or mentions of the book — with the name of the blurber and the publication or location of the blurber. What a treasure trove of information! These are people you may want to put on your media contact list! Here are people who liked the book (that is similar to your book) and wrote a blurb to recommend it and they let the author include it in their book! Perhaps they like the subject matter and want to read more books like it — your book! Perhaps they are an expert on the subject and want to read more about it — your book!

Do your online research to find the media contact information and their submission requirements and pitch.

Also, read the author's acknowledgements page of the book. Authors usually thank an agent or a publisher. Perhaps that agent or publisher could be YOUR new agent or publisher. They like your genre already, right? Send a pitch.

If you look inside a book or on the cover, you may find book awards that the book has earned. Book awards are great ways to get exposure for your books. Note the book award that a similar book has achieved and research the submission requirements for the award. Pitch your book for a possible book award! Be sure to note the submission deadlines in your research for book awards.

AMAZON AS A RESEARCH RESOURCE

We already discussed Amazon as a powerful social media resource for you to add your author page, reviews, recommended book lists, content and to connect with readers.

Amazon is also a terrific **resource** for you to research competitive book titles, find media contacts for your list, find reviewers to pitch, and to find possible publishers. Amazon is a resource to be used in your quest to publish your book as well as to market and promote it.

First understand that you have one of the most powerful databases of books at your fingertips. For example, let's say that you wrote an historical fiction book. What other books are published in your book's genre? This kind of research is very useful in helping you identify the categories and sub-categories where YOUR book belongs if you are a self-publisher, needed for your BISAC (Book Industry Standards and Communications) and CIP (Cataloging in Publication) data that you will need for your metadata, something imperative for wholesale buyers and libraries to discover. For now, however, we want to find the other books for sale in your category.

Here is what you do on Amazon:

- Go to the Amazon website. There are commands across the top of the website that as of this writing include "All" "Bestsellers" "Buy again" "Customer service" "Epic Deals" and "Books".
- Click on "All". You will see a drop-down list of commands.
- Select "Books". More drop-down lists.
- Select "Books" again. This will bring you to the "Books at Amazon" page.

Whoa! We told you that Amazon is an amazing resource. On the left side of the page, you will see a very detailed list of book categories. Are you geeking out with us? How cool is this?

Find your book category to discover the books in your genre and search the books as described above to identify new media contacts: book reviewers, journalists, potential blurb writers, book award organizations, potential agents and publishers.

This **Books at Amazon Page** is truly amazing. If you scroll down on the left-hand side, it even identifies book awards and the books that have won them recently (Booker Prize, Caldecott Medal, Eisner Award, etc.) Use Amazon as a social media channel and as an amazing resource!

So far in this chapter we have covered the idea of targeted social media marketing, the social media channel and resource that is Amazon, and some unique ways to find media contacts to pitch. Our last section in this chapter focuses on YOU. Specific ways that YOU are your resource to find new and productive ways to market and promote your book. We call it "Shake Your Tree."

SHAKE YOUR TREE FOR MARKETING IDEAS

Back in the day, 2008–2009, the best tip for authors to market their book was to add a signature line on their emails with their name, website, and book name with a link to each! Honestly, at that time, a signature line on an email was the slickest book marketing trick. It is still a good idea, but not the best idea by far. We believe that YOU are your best marketing idea. By "shake your tree" we mean: take a detailed looked at yourself, your family, and your friends, and answer the following questions.

What skills and talents do you have? (Feel free to use an additional piece of paper — wink, wink.)

What are some of the jobs you have held in your life?

What are the names of the companies where you have worked?

Are you great at photography?

What hobbies do you have?

What clubs have you joined?

Do your kids have special talents?

Does your partner have special talents?

Have you ever taught classes?

Where have you lived?

Like the "Brain Dump" exercise you completed previously, simply answer the questions above. Then go back and look at your answers. Are there any answers that might lead to creative book marketing? Here are a few examples of what we mean.

Still by Geraldine Donaher

We have a colleague who has a daughter who is a stand-up comedian. Her daughter was also great with TikTok. After reading her mother's book, titled *Still*, in which she learned that her mom had been a Catholic nun and fantasized about killing her husband, the daughter put together a funny TikTok. In the post, the daughter reads the book and flashes her (fake) amazement and horror at the surprises she learned while *Oops!...I did It Again* by Britney Spears plays in the background. It was so funny, yet provocative, that the TikTok post was widely shared and sales of *Still* skyrocketed.

The author of the book, Geraldine Donaher, recognized her daughter's talent and asked if she would create something for her. It was easy and a home run.

Claudine loves to speak in public. When promoting her first book, she searched for speaking gigs where she might also be able to sell her book and she found one. Although the gig paid a modest amount, she was featured on a local morning news program covering the Baby Expo Trade Show where she spoke. She was able to show her new book on the air and sales took off in the local morning show area. Home run!

Use the answers to your questions above to come up with unique ways to market your book. Again, we are not suggesting that you ask friends, family, and loved ones to buy your book. We are suggesting that you derive creative ideas from your own past and the skills and talents of those in your circle to market your book.

Distinctive Book Marketing Ideas

Perhaps your hobby is photography. Leverage your skill by using Instagram and Pinterest to their greatest potential — two social media channels that focus on pictures.

Let's say you like to teach. It is a very easy proposition to create and pitch an "Adult Class" to your local community college. Claudine once taught a class on social media marketing for books at Temple University's Adult Education program. She was paid to teach and, in the class brochure, she included the title of her book in her bio! The class brochure was mailed to thousands in the area.

Did you write a book about health and once work for a hospital? Get in touch with a colleague and ask to teach a class — hospitals and businesses are always looking to provide programs to the community on health topics.

You are now a writer! So, write! Ask your local paper to publish a guest opinion piece or lifestyle article on your expertise. Pitch magazines with article ideas that showcase your skills. Pitch blogs and websites with contributions! Your byline on such articles will include your book title and maybe even a link to your website!

Shake your tree to discover the marketing angles you may be able to explore to sell your book.

FINAL WORDS OF ADVICE

Book marketing is something that you can do for the entire life of your book. Our best advice to approach book marketing is in these pages. Take in a little bit at a time to keep from getting overwhelmed. Focus on your *Message, Audience, and Hook* and on your own interests and skills. Never forget that you know your book better than anyone. You are your best book marketing tool!

Distinctive Book Marketing Ideas

IS IT MARKETING OR PUBLICITY?

Tasks:	Circle ONE
Send galley copies to industry reviewers	Marketing or Publicity
Send galley copies to magazine book reviewers	Marketing or Publicity
Send galley copies to newspaper reviewers	Marketing or Publicity
Submit book to publishing catalogs	Marketing or Publicity
Send book postcard to libraries	Marketing or Publicity
Pitch radio, tv, newspapers to do a story	Marketing or Publicity
Pitch bloggers to review / do a story	Marketing or Publicity
Pitch podcasters to review / do a story	Marketing or Publicity
Radio, TV, Newspaper story interview is published	Marketing or Publicity
Blogger review / story on you or your book posted	Marketing or Publicity
Industry review on your book published	Marketing or Publicity
Goodreads author Q&A session published	Marketing or Publicity
Instagram live episode	Marketing or Publicity
Facebook live session	Marketing or Publicity
Advertisement for your book or a speaking gig	Marketing or Publicity
Book signing	Marketing or Publicity
Press Release creation	Marketing or Publicity
Press Release distribution	Marketing or Publicity
Author Bio release creation	Marketing or Publicity
Author Q&A creation	Marketing or Publicity

EXHIBITS

NewBuckPress
For Immediate Release

Contact: Publicist Name
xxxxxxxx@xxxxxxxx.xxx
(000) 000-0000

Motherhood – Making it a Bit Easier with Humor and Insider Secrets

New moms want to know what **really** works! They already know motherhood is hard, even though well meaning friends and family try to soften the reality by telling them 'it gets easier.' While raising her family on both the east coast in Pennsylvania and west coast in California, Claudine Wolk found that new moms were most concerned with three very practical issues: **how to get more sleep, how to get their baby on a schedule, and how to cope with the "mother-guilt" imposed by themselves and society at large.** She decided to attempt the impossible – make Motherhood a bit easier!

Her strategy - employ a little humor and lots of practical advice. "*Forget about playing nice and pretending that everything is normal and fine,*" Wolk says, "*Motherhood is hard! A new mom wants to know the insider secrets of new motherhood and what really works.*"

It Gets Easier!...and Other Lies We Tell New Mothers (New Buck Press, April 2008) presents a fun, honest, reflective and prescriptive guide for the new mother that will actually make new motherhood easier. Interviews with hundreds of moms and the author's personal experience, come together as this witty book breaks new ground with its honesty and humor mixed with practical strategies to give new moms a "leg-up" on the very often scary experience of motherhood. Through the conversation style, this book drives home the point that new moms are not alone and that there are some things they can try to make new motherhood a little more controllable and a lot more enjoyable. The **index** for easy refer-ence and the **resources** for further exploration creates a valuable book to be read, and then read again as new mother 'opportunities' arise.

Over a period of 12 years, Wolk interviewed hundreds of mothers from coast to coast, gained insight from participants of her workshops, and blended that valuable information with her own experience to develop practical strategies that are actually doable for a new mom – strategies that can actually work. Her "*new moms' tools*" including her famous baby schedule, workshops, websites, and many writings have helped thousands of women in their quest to expose the truth about motherhood and make it a bit easier!

Claudine Wolk is a nationally known speaker and columnist. In addition to writing on new mother issues with humor and honesty in newspapers, magazines, and websites, she is the creator of www.help4newmoms.com, a website designed specifically for helping new moms. Her workshops on all subjects of motherhood including "new mom issues" and "mothers getting back into the workforce" are fun, interactive and informative. Wolk lives in Bucks County, PA with her husband and her three children.

It Gets Easier!...and Other Lies We Tell New Mothers, published by New Buck Press retails for $12.95 and is available nationally at favorite local and online bookstores.

# # #

3949 Charter Club Drive, Doylestown, PA 18902
215-345-1992   www.help4newmoms.com

It Gets Easier!...
And Other Lies We Tell New Mothers
Claudine Wolk

Marketing Plan

PUBLICITY AND PROMOTION

Author will hire the publicity firm of Planned Television Arts. The author and the publicist will work in conjunction with the publisher on all marketing and publicity plans.

PRINT

Hybrid Mom magazine is nationally distributed in over 300 Gymboree Play & Music locations across the country and in Canada plus paid subscribers. *Hybrid Mom* magazine's current circulation is 100,000. The author's article "Desperate for Sleep? You must be a Mom" was highlighted on the front cover of the Spring 2008 issue. The author has an ongoing relationship with the editor of the magazine. The editor has agreed to feature *It Gets Easier!* in their magazine once published and in conjunction with the publisher. The author will continue to contribute articles for the magazine and is a featured blogger twice weekly on the *Hybrid Mom* website. HybridMom.com has a circulation of 200,000 and growing. The author's hyperlinked profile includes a link directly to the author's website.

Fit Pregnancy has agreed to run an article featuring Claudine and the book in the Dec/Jan 2009 issue in conjunction with the promotion and marketing department of the publisher. This date can be pushed back if needed to coincide with the release date.

Media kits will be sent to over 150+ national and regional long-lead and regional parenting magazines.

Media kits will be sent to over Top 250 Daily Newspapers targeting the Lifestyle Sections close to publishing date.

The author considers Mother's Day a golden opportunity to promote her work as a "mother expert." As a result of the current campaign, the author already has four local print interviews for Mother's Day, proving that the "help for new mother's story" is in demand.

Claudine will continue to promote her work and advice. The author is very passionate about her message that Motherhood can be made easier. To that end she continues to submit articles on all topics related to motherhood to local papers, national and regional magazines and websites.

Other organizations being pitched to speak, to carry the book and print articles/reviews are:

- YMCA – "New Mom" workshops
- Local Hospitals/Health & Wellness - "New Mom" workshops
- Grass Roots – Book Clubs
- MOPS – Local Doylestown Chapter
- Mamaslike.com – a website that features "mom" products
- Parents Magazine / American Baby (Meredith Corp.)
- Parenting / Babytalk (Bonnier Corp.)
- Working Woman Magazine
- About.com

RADIO

Dr. Laura program – national audience. Every week Dr. Laura highlights a book on her show. "On my radio program, I recommend relevant books which continue the discussions on topics that are significant to our lives: the sanctity of marriage, the welfare of our children, religion, and our values and moral fiber."

It Gets Easier! was selected for her March 10th nationally syndicated radio program resulting in approx 500 book sales through Amazon.com. The book is currently sitting on her popular website under the "Reading Corner" page where it can be purchased through Amazon with the click of a mouse. The producer of the *Dr. Laura Show* has agreed to promote and advertise the new, expanded version of the book upon publication.

ADVERTISING
Direct Mail

A direct mail campaign is planned to the purchased subscriber mailing list of leading publications including but not limited to: American Baby, Parenting, as well as the retail store chain Motherswork (Pea in a Pod.)

Additional mailings are also planned for the consumer market.

Newspaper advertising

The author has an eye-catching ad (created by the award winning Pneuma Books) that will run in local and national newspapers upon publication. The author will continue to run the ad at various locations to promote the book and the website.

Author Website

The author's website is dynamic and helpful for new moms as well as entertaining, much in the style of the book. Help4NewMoms.com has had 1,0748 hits in March, 7,152 hits in April and 8,795 hits in May. The author spends valuable time on the content of the website, making the website a favorite on Google searches on all topics motherhood. The author aggressively co-markets with other "mom" authors creating opportunities for more exposure and sales of the book.

The author's website offers free "new mom tools" that can be downloaded by the new mom. Each baby schedule has information about how to buy the book. Over 300 moms have downloaded the baby schedule and the numbers grow each day. The author's website is equipped to capture the emails of these "potential customers." Auto responder emails are sent periodically to these 'would-be' book buyers to remember to buy the book or pass specials along to friends.

The author will not continue sell the book on her website upon contract but will hyperlink the book to Amazon.com or the publisher's choice of outlet.

Author Newsletter

The Help4NewMoms newsletter goes out every two weeks to the author's website subscriber list of nearly 1,000 subscribers. It continues to grow with each speaking/signing engagement and each website promotion. The newsletter provides useful quick pieces of information to make a new mom smile or a quick tip to help her get through her day. The newsletter provides an easy way for the new mom to buy the book on the site and encourages purchase at local bookstores and other online bookstore sites.

Active Blog

The author will promote *It Gets Easier!* upon publication on the following active blogs.

The Help4NewMoms website has embedded in it the active Help4NewMoms blog which started in June 2007. The blog is similar to the book in content and humor but keeps new moms up to date on "new mom" issues as they occur in the headlines, online, and magazine articles, etc. The blog is available now at www.help4newmoms.blogspot.com.

The author is a member of popular "mom blog" communities where other Moms can find blogs that they may be interested in. Specifically, the author is a member of the two most popular blogs on the subject of motherhood, Mom Blogs, and BlogHer.com.

The author is a featured blogger for other websites as well, blogging on 21st century new mom issues for HybridMom.com, currently with a circulation of 200,000. The author is also a contributor to the websites Grumpymoms.com, Babyspot.com, and Mother-Talk.com. Wolk has a relationship with other "mom-bloggers" and her comments often appear on their heavily trafficked blogs:

- Babyonbored.blogspot.com (Stephanie Taylor-Wilder, author of *Sippy Cups Are Not for Chardonnay*
- Mom-101.blogspot.com (Liz Gumbinner, recently featured as a mom-blogger with Katie Couric on CBS)
- Mojomom.blogspot.com (Amy Tiemann, author of the award-winning book *Mojomom*)
- Mom2my6pack.blogspot.com (Dawn Meehan, over 83,601 profile views alone, creator of mamaslike.com)

The author is a frequent commentator on some of the most popular "mom-message boards" on the internet including:
- cafemom.com
- babyzone.com
- Justmommies.com
- ivillage.com
- msn.com
- urbanbaby.com
- discoveryheath.com
- Parents.com

Grass Roots Email Blast

myemma.com is a slick, dynamic on-line email marketing system. Upon publication, *It Gets Easier!* will be introduced to all personal, business, and key media affiliations through this marketing venue. Notices are sent for upcoming book signings, engagements, and appearances to keep the book fresh in the minds of those who know the author, have heard the author speak or have purchased the book. Each correspondence provides an easy way to share the email with a friend, forward the email, visit the author's website and purchase the book. This email system makes it easy to monitor the effectiveness of this marketing tool with a response system that reports statistics on each email campaign.

SPEAKING ENGAGEMENTS

Claudine Wolk understands the importance of meeting the readers and potential readers. She focuses intensive work on setting up speaking to groups, in bookstores, and through workshops.

Celebrate Mama — The author has been asked and has accepted the opportunity to promote at this annual expo. Celebrate Mama is an annual celebration bringing together products, services and information geared for and about motherhood. The author's book will be featured on the website at www.celebratemama.com which enjoys an average of 30,000 unique hits every 7 days! The author agrees to attend the conference each year to promote and sign books.

Bellies and Babies Maternity Expo, Indianapolis, IN Sept 6 — The author has been asked by the organizers of the expo, Motivated Mom Inc., to donate 10 signed copies of her books to this yearly show that attracts 5,000 attendees. Motivated Moms Inc. features the book on their website with a link to purchase books. The author is invited to submit her new, expanded title for next year.

Network Now, Doylestown — Author is invited to speak periodically. Network Now is a local women in business organization.

Bookstores and Libraries

- IBPA — use IBPA Target Marketing Catalogs to reach bookstores and libraries to support the launch
- Signings at bookstores in local areas and in areas where speaking is occurring — Philadelphia, Doylestown and Allentown
- Mailings to bookstores where media occurs or speaking is scheduled — full color flyer developed to use for notification

The author is actively sought to speak at local libraries and local business community groups. Most recently, the author has been invited to speak at The Friends of the Library Association upon publication. Tentatively, this engagement is scheduled for June 2009.

Hospitals

In honor of Mother's Day, the author promoted her work at a local maternity hospital in her hometown last month in May. The first 50 new Moms received a copy of the self-published book *It Gets Easier!* Pictures were taken and the local media notified. An interview for the Mother's Day giveaway promotion was secured. This type of promotion is effective and successful. The author will continue to market the book in this manner upon publication and expand the idea to additional cities.

Television

This is a strong visual story and one that reaches new moms, second time around moms, and grandparents. A national effort for TV interviews will also be implemented with Claudine as 'the expert' on many of the topics listed above with the direction of Planned Television Arts. This will begin with the launch in the local area at pub date and the national market for topics thereafter — continuing through the following seasons.

ENDORSEMENTS

A strong effort is underway to secure endorsements from key people with a vested and proven interest in the topic of new motherhood. The following shows the results with the 'requested' comment by those who have actively responded to date wanting a galley or book. These endorsement requests have gone out and we are expecting notification shortly.

Endorsement Received:
- The Dr Laura Show — Aired book through her March 10 national radio program. *It Gets Easier!* is on her website with a link to Amazon.com. Dr. Laura's producer will promote and advertise *It Gets Easier!* upon publication with a publisher.

- Susan Maushart (author of *Mask of Motherhood*) – Her endorsement is on the front cover of the self published version of *It Gets Easier!* She has further agreed to write the foreword for the new expanded version of the book.
- Amy Tiemann (Author of *Mojomom*) Her endorsement is on the back cover of the self-published version. She agrees to endorse the new, expanded version of the book.
- Suzanne Zoglio, PhD (Author of *Create a Life That Tickles Your Soul*) Her endorsement is on the indie cover. She agrees to endorse the new, expanded version of the book.
- Elizabeth Pantley (Author of the *New Mom Sleep Solution*, and 9 other books) will feature the author and book on her website www.help4newmoms under "parenting websites" and on her website www.pantley.com

Endorsements Actively Pursuing:
- Ann Crittenden (Author of *The Price of Motherhood*)
- Ariel Gore (Author of *Hip Mama* book and ezine)
- Ellen Goodman (*Boston Globe* columnist)
- Naomi Wolf (Author of *Misconceptions*)
- Nancy Grace (TV, mother of twins)
- Mary Matlin
- Jenny McCarthy (Ms. McCarthy received the book in April through her publicist)
- Kelly Ripa (Ms. Ripa has received the book personally through her Nanny)
- Rachel Ray (Pitched story through her producer at *The Rachel Ray Show*)
- Jenna Elfman (Ms. Elfman has received the book through her publicist)
- Naomi Watts (Ms. Watts has received the book through her publicist)

VOLUME PURCHASE

Toys R Us — The book buyer for Toys R Us, Jessica Simonson is currently reviewing the book for inclusion in Babies R Us product line.

MothersWork — Kim Holtzman, the accessories buyer, at MothersWork is currently reviewing the book for their inclusion in their product line in their stores and online. MothersWork owns Mimi, A Pea in the Pod, and Destination Maternity.

Author's husband is a CFO at Johnson & Johnson. He is in the process of working with their marketing group to purchase the book as a promotional item for their OB/GYN and Pediatric doctor clients.

I See the Sun Books

Life in different countries told from a child's point of view. *I See the Sun* is a series of bi-lingual picture books, each focused on one country and one day in the life of one child with a story told from the child's perspective. Every book provides a unique introduction to the culture, family life and language of one particular country in a way that is age-appropriate and sensitive to each culture. The countries represented in these books are ones in which the author has spent a considerable amount of time, not merely as a tourist, but immersed in the environment and living with families who have opened their homes and their hearts to her. Includes country facts and glossary for extended learning.

Dedie King is a former Peace Corps volunteer in Nepal and taught school in Katmandu and Bandipur. She remains a world traveler and currently practices Taoist acupuncture. Illustrator Judith Inglese combines photography and drawing in her illustrations. She also designs and fabricates ceramic murals for public spaces.

For ages 5+ ♦ 40 fully illustrated pages ♦ 8.5 x 8.5
Paperback | $12.95 US ♦ Hardcover | $17.95 US
Author: Dedie King   Illustrator: Judith Inglese

"...Move over *Peter Rabbit* and *Hop on Pop!* Providing a learning tool with recognizable characters and surroundings... now that's a true (and useful) gift of education."
— Terry Hong, *Book Dragon*, Smithsonian Asian Pacific American Program

I See the Sun in Myanmar (Burma) English and Burmese ♦ ISBN: 9781935874201

I See the Sun in Mexico
English and Spanish ♦ ISBN: 9781935874140
Foreword Book of the Year Honorable Mention - 2012

I See the Sun in Russia
English and Russian ♦ ISBN: 9781935874089

I See the Sun in Afghanistan
English and Dari (Afghan Farsi) ♦ ISBN: 9780981872087
Foreword Book of the Year Finalist

I See the Sun in Nepal
English and Nepalese (Devanagari) ♦ ISBN: 9780981872094

I See the Sun in China
English and Mandarin Chinese ♦ ISBN: 9780981872056
Learning® Magazine Teachers' Choice℠ Award for the Family
Creative Child Magazine Preferred Book Award

Note regarding Foreign Rights/Translation: The English in the *I See the Sun* books can be translated into another language OR a third language can be added to the layout.
www.iseethesunbooks.com

Exhibits

GET YOUR BOOK SEEN AND SOLD

Book Marketing Must-Do's

☐ Book Reviews - Pre-Publication
　　**Book Industry Reviews: Submit 4-5 Months in Advance
　　**Media Reviews
　　Colleague Reviews to Place on **Amazon, BookBub, Goodreads

☐ Internet Promotion - Pre-Publication / Launch Day
　　Sites that offer blog posts, interviews, mentions for a fee: **BookTrib, WOW, WhizzBooks **Ads: **Facebook Ad, Amazon Ad**
　　**Ads: Genre Specific Sites
　　Paid Promotion on Book Sites: **Bookbub: New Releases Program, Goodreads
　　Paid Mentions by Influencers: **Fiverr, Instagram, Facebook

☐ Media Outreach - Pre-Publication: 4 weeks in advance
　　** Pitch to Radio, TV, Newspaper, Magazines: Review, Interview, Mention ** Pitch to Podcasts for Interview

☐ Media Outreach - Post Publication: Ongoing
　　** Pitch to Radio, TV, Newspaper, Magazines: Review, Interview, Mention ** Pitch to Podcasts for Interview

☐ Distributor Promotion - Pre-publication
　　** Ingram Spark ie. Sales to Libraries / Bookstore - Catalog Placement
　　** Add Title to Sites For Pre-Order - Months in Advance

　　　Amazon: Deadline _____
　　　iBooks: Deadline _____
　　　KOBO: Deadline _____
　　　IngramSpark _____

☐ Author Social Media
　　** website: www.your **name.com**
　　** social media channels: pick 2 that align w/ interests/skills
　　** Amazon Author Page
　　** Goodreads Author Page
　　** Email Signature: add link to book sale site

☐ Author Ground Game
　　** Speaking Engagements (Live or Online)
　　** Article Writing Submission on Genre
　　** Review Books in your Genre on Amazon

TOOLS NEEDED TO PROMOTE YOUR BOOK:

MEDIA KIT ITEMS
- Press Release
- Author Biography
- Book One Page
- Endorsement Page
- Interview Q&A
- Cover Letter Pitches
- Media Contact List

GET YOUR BOOK SEEN AND SOLD

Book Marketing Folder Process

Book Marketing is finding ways to connect the people who desire your message with YOUR book. It can be fun and creative— and a bit overwhelming— so many ideas, so many choices.
To keep your book marketing organized and efficient, try this tried-and-true book marketing file folder organization process.

FOLDER TITLE	WHAT TO PUT IN THE FOLDER & WHY
Book Distribution	Book Distribution is Book Marketing Put your research and decisions on book distribution here
Book Cover	Your Book Cover is Book Marketing Put vendors, book cover ideas, back cover copy ideas & Amazon Book Info here
Book Promotion - BookBub	BookBub offers reasonably priced, targeted promotion and ads to target audiences New releases, Featured Deal, Ads
Book Promotion - Other	Every other promotion/ad idea you research, consider or try is kept in this folder BookBub promotion has its own folder.
Publisher Rocket	Must-Have Software by Kindlepreneur Identify Categories, Keywords, Competition for Book Pages, Promotion & Media Kit
Book Review Outreach	Pre & Post Publication Book Review Program Details Your Plan to Gather Reviews
Book Marketing Plan	Your Formal List of Book Marketing Tasks
Media Kit	Notes for Creating Media Kit Items Press Release, Author Bio, Sell Sheet, Endorsements, Cover Letter Pitch, Q&A
Media Contacts	Collect the Media Contacts You Plan to Pitch Magazine, Newspaper, TV, Radio, Websites, Podcasts, Industry
Social Media	Details, Notes and Logins for Two Social Media Channels Instagram, Pinterest, Goodreads, Facebook, LinkedIn, TikTok, YouTube
Business	A Book Marketer owns a business. Keep business related details in this folder Logins, passwords, etc.
How-To	A Book Marketer will be learning many new things Keep instructions in one go-to place.

ABOUT THE AUTHORS

Claudine's and Julie's Publishing Stories

Some people have called us Book Shepherds; others have called us Book Marketers, Publicists, Authors, Writers, Editors, Proofreaders, Designers, Photographers and Publishers. Between the two of us, we have covered it all (or most of it)!

We each have an individual "book publishing" story. We are sharing these stories to help you to get to know us a bit and understand that we truly know what you are going through (and are about to go through).

Claudine's Publishing Story

Once upon a time there was a woman who had a message. She wanted to share that message with other women in a book. The year was 2007 and she was living in California, the result of a cross-country transfer with her husband's company. Quite a change. She had three young kids with her — ages 3, 7, and 11 — and she did not know a soul in California. At that time, she was in the habit of writing down tips and observations that she had learned from other mothers and experts on the topic of motherhood. She wanted to share this fabulous, honest and helpful information. Since she was now on the west coast, she felt that it was the perfect opportunity to get additional advice from women and experts on the other side of the country.

When she discovered that a family friend had gotten a full-blown publishing contract with a traditional publisher after a few weeks of pitching her manuscript, it lit a healthy fire. After months of rejection from traditional publishers and agents, she taught herself how to self-publish with the help of Dan Poynter's famous guide, *The Self-Publishing Manual*. When the book distributor, Midpoint Books, sent her the email with an attached contract to distribute her book, she felt like "Rudy" from the movie of the same title, when he learned that he had finally been accepted to Notre Dame. The happiness, relief and excitement were overwhelming. Her book was published in 2008. Later, a traditional publishing company contracted her to write three more chapters and then re-released the book under their imprint in 2009.

Claudine believes there is nothing like getting your message out there and hopes that this book offers you the help that you need to have your "Rudy" moment. You have a message. You want to share it. The authors' hope is that you find a way to publish and successfully market it with the help of this book. This is YOUR first step in achieving your goal, regardless of YOUR publishing journey. Enjoy it and go get 'em!

Julie's Story

Julie began working with books and writers while still in college as the founder of Womanchild Press. For several years Womanchild Press published chapbooks, broadsides, and an annual poetry magazine. Each publication was created one letter at a time, using metal type and a 19th century treadle-operated letterpress. Although the technological transition from letterpress to computer-generated materials was gradual, her dedication to quality and perfection has remained consistent. Later, she established Satya House Publications with the catchphrase "Ignorance is not bliss, knowledge is." Satya House has published numerous fiction and non-fiction trade books, as well as a series of bi-lingual picture books, the *I See the Sun in....* series, which introduces children to life and language in different countries. Books published by Satya House have won numerous awards and have been featured in magazines and websites around the world.

Julie currently provides a range of creative services to writers and small publishers. She is passionate about words and the ways they can be combined to transmit complex transformative ideas. Design services

Why Us?

are available to publishers, businesses, entrepreneurs, and self-publishing writers nationwide. She also provides copyediting and proofreading, as well as consulting on marketing, publicity, and distribution. She loves to support writers and emerging entrepreneurs in making the transition to their next level of development. In 2021, she established Lost Valley Press as an imprint of Satya House Publications. Lost Valley Press is a hybrid publisher, offering many of the benefits of a traditional publisher, but without the constraints that frequently accompany them.

www.ingramcontent.com/pod-product-compliance
Lightning Source LLC
LaVergne TN
LVHW052032080426
835513LV00018B/2294